ADVENT/CHRISTMAS

**INTERPRETING
THE LESSONS OF
THE CHURCH YEAR**

MARK ALLAN POWELL

**PROCLAMATION 5
SERIES A**

FORTRESS PRESS   MINNEAPOLIS

PROCLAMATION 5
Interpreting the Lessons of the Church Year
Series A, Advent/Christmas

Scripture quotations, unless otherwise noted, are from the New Revised Standard Version of the Bible, copyright © 1989 by the Division of Christian Education of the National Council of the Churches of Christ in the United States of America. Used by permission.

Cover and interior design: Spangler Design Team

Library of Congress Cataloging-in-Publication Data

Proclamation 5 : interpreting the lessons of the church year.
     p.   cm.
    Contents: ser. a [1] Epiphany / Pheme Perkins. [2] Holy week /
Robert H. Smith. [3] Advent/Christmas / Mark Allan Powell.
[4] Lent / Cain Hope Felder.
    ISBN 0-8006-4178-7 (ser. A, Epiphany) — ISBN
0-8006-4180-9 (ser. A, Holy week) — ISBN 0-8006-4177-9
(ser. A, Advent/Christmas) — ISBN 0-8006-4179-5 (ser. A, Lent)
    1. Bible—Homiletical use.   2. Bible—Liturgical lessons, English.
BS534.5.P765   1992
251—dc20   92-22973
                                                                                   CIP

The paper used in this publication meets the minimum requirements of American National Standard for Information Services—Permanence of Paper for Printed Library Materials, ANSI Z329.48-1984. ∞™

Manufactured in the U.S.A.   AF 1-4177

96   95   94   93   92   1   2   3   4   5   6   7   8   9   10

CONTENTS

FOR MY PASTORS:

William Kaiser
Norman Kieffer
Carl Ruch
Ron Birk
Robert Otterstad
John Schwarz
August Wenzel
David Doerfler
Robert Lehmann
Robert Swanger
Lloyd Volkmar
Delmas Luedke
Henry Flathmann
Jim Mauney
Al Debelak

First Sunday in Advent

Lutheran	Roman Catholic	Episcopal	Common Lectionary
Isa. 2:1-5	Isa. 2:1-5	Isa. 2:1-5	Isa. 2:1-5
Rom. 13:11-14a	Rom. 13:11-14a	Rom. 13:8-14	Rom. 13:11-14
Matt. 24:37-44	Matt. 24:37-44	Matt. 24:37-44	Matt. 24:36-44

FIRST LESSON: ISAIAH 2:1-5

Micah 4:1-4 contains a slightly different form of this oracle. Scholars debate which of the two versions is the original; many believe both to derive from another, more primitive source.

The oracle as a whole proclaims a wondrous act of God that the prophet is certain will occur in the future. Whether the prophet believes this future lies within or beyond the bounds of history is, again, a matter of debate. The oracle is dated too early to be affected by apocalyptic categories. It is, however, unquestionably eschatological insofar as it describes a promised future in terms that impinge directly on life in the present.

Verse 1 provides the heading not only for this oracle but for much of what follows. Apparently this oracle once stood at the beginning of an independent collection addressed to Judah/Jerusalem. The reference to the prophet *seeing* (as opposed to hearing) the word is interesting, reflective perhaps of the visionary medium through which the revelation was received.

The oracle itself follows an indicative/imperative pattern in which a descriptive statement of God's activity (vv. 2-4) is followed by an exhortation concerning the proper response to this activity (v. 5). Such patterns are typical throughout the Bible and become a staple form of gospel/law proclamation in the New Testament ("The kingdom of God has come near; repent, and believe . . ." [Mark 1:15]).

In this case, the descriptive statement of God's activity concerns a matter that is yet to occur: the exaltation of Zion above all other mountains (cf. Ps. 48:2; Isa. 40:3-5; Ezek. 40:2; Zech. 14:10). Some interpreters think the prophet means this literally. In the future Mt. Zion, which is not of a particularly impressive elevation, will be made to grow miraculously until it becomes the highest mountain in the world. Such a topographical wonder would certainly generate pilgrimages from far and wide.

The prophet's desires would all be met, however, if only the metaphorical sense of his oracle was fulfilled: recognition of Yahweh as the God of all the earth (cf. 1 Kings 8:41-43; Ps. 22:27-31; Isa. 25:6-10; 45:22-23; Jer. 3:17). The day will come, this prophet is sure, when all people will acknowledge the God of Israel and will desire to walk in the ways of the Lord. People from all nations will come to worship at the Lord's house, and the *torah* ("instructions," v. 3) will go out from Jerusalem to be received by all the world.

Once this occurs, justice will prevail. The Lord will arbitrate disputes and all nations will have a common standard (i.e., the word of God) to determine what is right. Significantly, this establishment of justice will lead in turn to an unprecedented reign of peace. The usual battle cry to turn agricultural implements into weapons (Joel 3:10) will be reversed. Justice, the prophet thinks, is an indispensable prerequisite for peace, but peace is also an inevitable consequence of justice.

The oracle is notable for its lack of imperialistic tendencies. It has more in common with the traditions of Abraham than with those of David. There is no thought here of Israel subduing or conquering the nations. Rather, Israel will fulfill the purpose of its election by becoming a source of blessing for all the families of the earth (Gen. 12:2-3).

The oracle, furthermore, does not offer its picture of the future as a pious hope or idyllic dream, but as an assured reality. Therefore, the prophet concludes with the exhortation, "O house of Jacob, come, let us walk in the light of the Lord." This is not, as one commentator puts it, an appeal "so that the longed-for age of world peace may be hastened in." Israel's faithfulness to the covenant does not bring about the establishment of God's universal reign. The prophet's reasoning, in terms of cause and effect, is precisely the opposite: realization that the eventual establishment of God's universal reign is a given should provide Israel with the confidence and trust necessary to accept that reign even now. If someday even the most pagan nations will obey the Torah, then surely privileged Israel should be able to do so.

SECOND LESSON: ROMANS 13:11-14

These verses conclude an ethical section of Paul's letter to the Romans that encompasses all of chapters 12 and 13. Along with 12:1-2, they provide the eschatological framework within which everything else in these two chapters is to be understood. In the preceding verses Paul has discussed how Christians are to behave toward one another (12:3-13), toward enemies (12:14-21), toward the state (13:1-7), and toward "neighbors" in general (13:8-10). His instruction may be summarized in a word: love, which is the fulfilling of the law (13:10). Paul began this instruction by urging disassociation from the present age (12:1-2); he now concludes it by asserting that the present age is drawing (and, in some sense, has drawn) to a close.

Paul believes his readers will regard his instructions as all the more urgent if they are aware of the *kairos* (v. 11)—that is, the appointed time, the moment of destiny—in which they live. And what time is it? Time, he says, to "wake from sleep." In 1 Thess. 5:4-8, Paul uses this metaphor the way it is also used in our Gospel lesson for today—as a call to vigilance. The point here, however, seems to be simply that a new age is dawning (cf. the baptismal song in Eph. 5:14). In v. 12, Paul uses the passage of night into day as an image for understanding the transition from the old age to the new one.

English Bibles translate the key words in v. 12 differently: day is "at hand" (KJV, RSV, NASB), "near" (NEB, NRSV), "almost here" (NIV). The Greek word *eggidzō* can be interpreted as meaning either that day has already arrived or that day is about to dawn. The difference is significant. If Paul means to say that the new age of salvation is already here, then he must be referring to the age initiated by the death and resurrection of Christ. If he means that the new age is soon to appear, he must be thinking of the ultimate salvation that will come only with the parousia.

The latter interpretation is better. Paul sometimes does speak of salvation as a present reality (2 Cor. 6:2), but he has just said here that "salvation is nearer to us now than when we became believers" (v. 11), implying that salvation still lies in the future. Paul's assertion that it is already time to wake from sleep does not imply that the new day has already dawned. In Paul's world, most people rose before daybreak. The image, then, is this: the new age of salvation is coming just as surely as day follows night. In fact, it is so close to arriving that it is already time to get up and do what one must do to greet the day.

One thing that people do when they arise is get dressed. So, Paul continues to draw on his new-day metaphor by saying it is now time to put on those things appropriate for the day. The expression "works of darkness" in v. 12 does not refer only to things done under the cover of dark, for the worst of sins are often committed in broad daylight. Rather, "works of darkness" refers to whatever will be inappropriate in the new era of salvation. The time to stop doing such things is now.

The image of "putting off" (cf. Eph. 4:22, 25; Col. 3:8; Heb. 12:1; James 1:21; 1 Pet. 2:1) and "putting on" (cf. Gal. 3:27; Eph. 4:24; Col. 3:10-12; 1 Thess. 5:8; 1 Pet. 4:1) is probably reflective of a baptismal ceremony. Christians discarded their old garments to be baptized and then, coming up out of the water, were clothed anew in white robes. Paul departs somewhat from the strictly baptismal imagery to introduce a military theme. The Christian is to put on the "armor of light" (cf. 2 Cor. 6:7; 10:4; Eph. 6:11, 13-17; 1 Thess. 5:8). This juxtaposition is not as incongruous as it may seem to some readers today. Baptism prepares us for a life of conflict, not passivity. The Greek word for *armor* here refers to a soldier's offensive equipment (spear, sword, etc.) as well as to defensive coverings.

(Some interpreters may note an unintentional parallel with the first lesson at this point. Isaiah sees the eschatological age as a time for the destruction of conventional weapons, as in v. 2:4; Paul sees it as a time for the taking up of spiritual ones. The connection is further enhanced by the use of the word *light* in both Isa. 2:5 and Rom. 13:12.)

Paul offers specific examples only for what is to be put off, not for what is to be put on (but see v. 14), probably because he has already listed the kinds of behavior that are appropriate to the new age in the two chapters preceding our lesson for today. In any case, his specific examples of works of darkness are listed as three pairs of synonyms: reveling and drunkenness (cf. Gal. 5:21; 1 Pet. 4:3); debauchery and licentiousness; and quarreling and jealousy (cf. 1 Cor. 3:3; 2 Cor. 12:20; Gal. 5:20).

A word must be said about "debauchery." The word used here is the Greek word for *bed* (*koitēs*), a word that is sometimes used as a euphemism for sexual intercourse (cf. Heb. 13:4) but that is never (except here) used for sexual immorality. It would be wrong to suppose that Paul believes all sexual relations should be put off as the new day of salvation dawns. Rather, the word derives its unique connotation by being paired with *licentiousness* (cf. 2 Cor. 12:21; Gal. 5:19; 1 Thess. 4:3; Eph. 4:19; 1 Pet. 4:3; 2 Pet. 2:18). When we hear a modern person say, "We need to rid our society of sex and filth," we realize that he or she probably does not want to get rid of all sex, but only the aspects or forms of sex that he or she considers filthy. Nevertheless, the prudishness evident in using an innocent word for sexual relations in such a context is revealing, as indeed it is here of Paul.

Finally, Paul sums up his entire exhortation in a phrase: put on the Lord Jesus Christ (v. 14). To do so means, negatively, to "make no provision for the flesh, to gratify its desires." Positively, it means to "present your bodies as a living sacrifice, holy and acceptable to God" (12:1) and to be "transformed by the renewing of your minds" (12:2). Paul has come full circle back to the eschatological context in which he began. By putting off the works of darkness, we cease to be conformed to this world, and by putting on Christ, we are transformed for the new age that is about to dawn.

In Gal. 3:27, Paul says that in baptism we already have put on Christ. Most likely, then, what he envisions here is a daily renewal and affirmation of what has already occurred in baptism. This is done, furthermore, in anticipation of the ultimate salvation that we are yet to receive, the sure and certain hope that is close enough even now to command our full attention.

GOSPEL: MATTHEW 24:37-44

These verses probably derive from the so-called Q source (cf. Luke 17:26-40) although similar thought occurs also in Mark 13:33-37. In Matthew's Gospel, they have become part of the "eschatological discourse," the last of five great speeches delivered by Jesus (chaps. 5–7; 9:35—10:42; 13:1-52; 17:24—18:35; chaps. 24–25). The immediate context for the verses, then, includes the whole of chapters 24 and 25.

The tone for the sayings is set by 24:36, where Jesus declares that no one—not humans, not angels, not even the Son himself—knows the day or the hour when heaven and earth will pass away (v. 35). For this reason, vigilance must be constant. For the Christian, every day and every hour is charged with eschatological significance. ✓

Modern readers may think of "the days of Noah" as a time when people became so sinful that God regretted ever having created them (Gen. 6:5-6). But this is not the point of Jesus' allusion to those days in vv. 37-39. There is nothing evil about "eating and drinking," nothing wicked about "marrying and giving in marriage." Rather, the point is that people in Noah's time were so absorbed with the routines of everyday life that they failed to notice the salvation/judgment of God taking shape in their midst. The spiritual danger envisioned here is not iniquity but apathy. The coming of the Son of man will disrupt the pleasant routines of those who have not taken such an eventuality into account, who have lived as though the future would never arrive.

Jesus goes on to indicate, however, that this will not be true for all. With intentional inclusivity, Jesus refers to both men and women who will be "taken," as well as to men and women who will be "left." Christians often assume the former fate is desirable, and this may be correct (cf. 24:31). Elsewhere in Matthew, however, those who are taken, or "plucked up," are likened to weeds that are destined for the fire (13:30, 40-42; 15:13). If this is the case, we should all hope to be "left behind"! In any case, there is no thought here of a rapture or rescue of faithful Christians in advance of the end.

The remaining verses (42-44) specify the conclusion to be drawn from the fact that we cannot know when the Son of man will come: we should watch (v. 42) and be ready (v. 44). What does it mean to watch and be ready? Jesus clarifies this by telling four parables in the material that follows (24:45—25:46). In this lesson for today, we receive only a clue. For those who are not watchful and ready, the coming of the Son of man will be like having one's house broken into by a thief (v. 43). This cannot mean that keeping watch will enable us to stave off the Son of man's approach, as we would that of a thief. Nor can it mean that keeping watch will enable us to predict the time of his coming, since this is unknowable (v. 36). Rather, for those who watch, the coming of the Son of man need not be regarded as a threat. To be ready means that one does not experience the coming of the Son of man as an intrusion. The Son of man comes as Lord to those who are ready (v. 42) and as thief to those who are not (v. 43).

Life in the present should be determined by what we know of the future. There are details about the future that we cannot know, but the establishment of God's reign is certain. As Matthew's Gospel makes repeatedly clear, God's reign is in some sense already established ("come near"—3:2; 4:17; 10:7). In the same way, those who await the coming of the Son of man may live as though he were already here. Before Jesus finishes his eschatological discourse, he will reveal that this is in fact the case: the Son of man comes to people even now in ways that are unrecognized (25:31-46). God's future has a way of breaking into the present, but for those who are watchful and ready, this is a welcome disruption.

REFLECTIONS

The season of Advent celebrates the coming of Christ to us in all three tenses: past, present, and future. Today the focus is on Christ's future advent, on promises and hopes yet to be fulfilled. All three lessons for today proclaim that God's people have a future and that awareness of this future is significant for life in the present. Knowing that God holds the future saves us from cynical resignation on the one hand, and from self-righteous ambition (cf. James 4:13-15) on the other. Our present is determined by God's future!

Yet eschatological awareness is not strong in mainstream Christianity today. In most churches, few members actually entertain a lively expectation of the end and those who do may be thought a bit odd. Theological interest in such matters has come to be associated with faulty exegetes and rabble-rousers, with popular preachers who set dates and then explain why the timetable was not met. In fact, perceptive parishioners may note, even the authors of today's lessons seem to fit this embarrassing description: Christ did not return with the expediency Paul expected; Jerusalem did not become the beacon of peace and justice anticipated by Isaiah.

Two points are significant here: (1) With regard to God's promises, certainty of fulfillment is more important than timing. The Gospel lesson is clear about this; Isaiah and Paul would agree as well. (2) The future, even if far off, impinges upon us now, drawing us in, so to speak, with proleptic moments of eschatological consummation. Jesus *will come* to us, Matthew's Gospel says. Also, when two or three gather in his name they may discover he is already there in their midst (18:20). He may be found in children (18:5), in bread and wine (26:26-28), in the needy (25:31-46). He is coming at the end of the age, but he is also with us always until that time (28:20). These experiences of Christ's present-tense advent may be what encourage Christians like Paul to speak of God's future as something that is both still to come and yet already here. The tragedy is when, like men and women in the days of Noah, people are too absorbed with ordinary pursuits to notice the moment of *kairos* when it arrives.

At this particular time of year, potentially distracting ordinary pursuits abound. They include shopping, wrapping presents, mailing cards, baking cookies—in short, getting ready for Christmas in ways that do not necessarily include getting ready for Christ. The task of

11

the preacher on this first Sunday in Advent is to stir people's souls so that they will be as excited by the coming of Christ as they are by the coming of Christmas. We know that Christmas is coming, and we devote ourselves even now to preparing for that day. We know that Christ is coming too.

Second Sunday in Advent

Lutheran	Roman Catholic	Episcopal	Common Lectionary
Isa. 11:1-10	Isa. 11:1-10	Isa. 11:1-10	Isa. 11:1-10
Rom. 15:4-13	Rom. 15:4-9	Rom. 15:4-13	Rom. 15:4-13
Matt. 3:1-12	Matt. 3:1-12	Matt. 3:1-12	Matt. 3:1-12

FIRST LESSON: ISAIAH 11:1-10

This oracle is situated within a series of prophecies (chaps. 2–12) that address concerns of Judah and Jerusalem brought on by the Syro-Ephraimite War in the latter half of the eighth century B.C. Some scholars think the oracle itself is from a later time and has been edited to fit the context. In any case, we are expected to receive this text as words of promise spoken to God's people at a time when all hope seemed lost. The words are clearly messianic and eschatological. As such, they pick up on themes already introduced in 2:1-5 (our first lesson for last week) and in 9:2-7 (the first lesson for Christmas Day).

The first verse presents a wonderful image: a green shoot springs to life from a dead stump. Such biological miracles occur because, even though the stump of a tree may be dead, new growth can stem from buried but still living roots. This image is presented in deliberate contrast to that of Isa. 10:33-34, where the judgment of God is likened to the felling of a mighty forest. The theme of these two images combined is eminently biblical: God humbles the mighty and exalts the lowly (cf. Luke 14:11; 18:14).

Isaiah tells us that the stump in his illustration is to be identified with Jesse, the father of David. We are not told with whom the shoot is to be identified but are left to infer this from the description offered in vv. 2-5.

The shoot from the stump of Jesse will not only be a descendant of David, but like David will also be one upon whom the Spirit of the Lord rests (cf. 1 Sam. 16:13; 2 Sam. 23:2). Verses 2-3a describe this charismatic endowment in terms that the church has used to describe the sevenfold gifts of the Spirit sought by believers at their Confirmation or Affirmation of Baptism. The *Lutheran Book of Worship*, for example, lists them as wisdom, understanding, counsel, might, knowledge, fear of the Lord, and joy in God's presence. The ruler who possesses such gifts will not have to rely on what his own eyes see or on what his own ears hear, for the Spirit will enable him to transcend the normal limitations of human perception (v. 3bc). Thus, he will be aptly equipped to carry out his most important function: judgment on behalf of the poor and meek (v. 4). His word will destroy what is arrogant (preferred textual variant to the NRSV's "earth" in 4c) and wicked. He will succeed not only because he is exceptionally gifted but also because he embodies the divine qualities of righteousness and faithfulness (v. 5).

Who can this remarkable person be? Some interpreters guess Ahaz; others, Josiah; but neither of these seem likely. As Calvin pointed out long ago, none of the Davidic kings, not even David himself, ever lived up to such a portrait. Accordingly, the image of the shoot from the stump of Jesse is probably intended as a metaphor that remains fluid, lending itself to reinterpretation. Thus, the image remains a sign of hope and can be read as a reference to one whose name the prophet did not know, but whose coming was assured by the promise of God.

Christians believe they do know this person's name. Isaiah's oracle reads like a near-perfect description of Jesus: descended from David (Matt. 1:1), endowed with the Spirit (Matt. 3:16), extraordinarily gifted (Matt. 28:18), defender of the poor (Luke 6:20) and meek (Matt. 5:5), paradigm of righteousness (Matt. 3:15; Phil. 1:11) and faithfulness (John 13:1; Heb. 2:17), and so on. In our second lesson for today, Paul takes this identification of "the root of Jesse" with Jesus to be self-evident (Rom. 15:12).

But even Christians must regard the latter half of Isaiah's oracle as unfulfilled. We have here, in vv. 6-9, a description of life as it will be when the promised one's work is complete. The mythological images of animals living at peace (vv. 6-7) are intended to describe in some ultimate sense the effect of the judgment mentioned in v. 4: the weak no longer need to fear the strong. Luther notes, poignantly, that the images suggest such peace is accomplished by the mighty becoming like the lowly, rather than the other way around. The overall picture, of course, is one of paradise regained, a popular notion that conceives of the end of time as being similar to its beginning. Life as it was intended to be in Eden is recovered—and improved! This time even the serpents will be harmless (v. 8)! All this will happen when (but not until) the whole earth is filled with the knowledge of the Lord (v. 9). For the time being, the spreading of that knowledge remains our principal task.

Verse 10 is not part of this oracle as such but is intended to serve as a transition that links 11:1-9 with what follows. It does this by citing the key words *Jesse* (cf. 11:1) and *signal* (cf. 11:12). Paul quotes this verse in our second lesson for today (Rom. 15:12), but his main interest is in its mention of "the nations" (Gentiles).

SECOND LESSON: ROMANS 15:4-13

The context for this pericope is Paul's exhortation to "strong" Christians to welcome those who are weak in faith, a point he has been making since 14:1. The "weak" Christians he has in mind are certain Jewish believers who observe dietary and ritualistic customs based on a very strict interpretation of the Bible; the strong include Gentile converts along with a few Jewish Christians (like Paul) who know better. In Paul's view, only the latter really understand the freedom of the gospel. But here Paul considers the issue in light of another, overriding concern: the unity of the church, which is always a matter of great importance to him (Romans 12; 1 Corinthians 12). As a result, we find in today's text a beautiful example of Paul practicing what he preaches in 14:1-12. With grace and with style, he urges acceptance of persons with whom he himself does not agree.

Verses 4-6, with which the lectionary text begins, are actually parenthetical to the main point Paul is trying to make, namely that Christians should follow Christ's example of practicing self-denial for the sake of others. In v. 3 he quoted a scriptural text (Ps. 69:9) to illustrate this, and now he reminds his readers that all of the Scriptures were "written for our instruction" (v. 4; cf. 1 Cor. 9:10, 10:6; 2 Tim. 3:16-17). To be specific, the Scriptures offer steadfastness and encouragement, which in turn lead us to hope (v. 5). They can do this because the God to which they testify is "the God of steadfastness and encouragement" (v. 5) and "the God of hope" (v. 13). Thus, the Scriptures impart to us God's own qualities.

Paul's prayer is that this divine grace will allow us to live in harmony or, literally, to "be of one mind" (v. 5). The latter expression is a favorite of Paul's (Rom. 12:16; 2 Cor. 13:11; Phil. 2:2, 5; 4:2) and is not meant to discourage differences of opinion. In fact, Paul has just told these readers that on some matters it is alright for "all to be fully convinced in their own minds" (Rom. 14:5). Despite such disagreements, however, believers can share one mind "in accordance with Christ Jesus" (v. 5). The "one mind" we are to have is the mind of Christ (cf. Phil. 2:5-8), who has become a servant (v. 8) and a bearer of the mercy of God (v. 9). If we share this mind-set, we will welcome one another with the same gracious hospitality that Christ has shown to us (v. 7).

Having made this point, Paul concludes with a catena of scriptural quotations and a benediction. The Scripture readings draw from all three portions of the Old Testament (Law, Prophets, Writings) and all speak of Gentiles as included among God's people. Verse 9b is from Ps. 18:49 and 2 Sam. 22:50; v. 10 is from Deut. 32:43; v. 11 is from Ps. 117:1; and v. 12 is from Isa. 11:10. The quotations cited in verses 10 and 12 differ markedly from their counterparts in Deuteronomy and Isaiah in our English Bibles because most English translations rely more heavily on the Hebrew text than on the Greek Septuagint used by Paul.

The first three quotations focus specifically on worship. This, for Paul, is the reason the unity of the church is so important. I find that surprising. I would have expected his practical rationale to appeal to something else, such as effectiveness in mission. But here at least, Paul is concerned that if the church is not unified, God will not be adequately praised. Looking back at vv. 5-6, we see now that the reason we are to have one mind is so that we can glorify God with one voice. Again, Christ's welcome of us was for "the glory of God" (v. 7). And, again, Gentiles who realize Christ came as a servant to the very ones they call weak should glorify God for such mercy (vv. 8-9).

The final Scripture lesson Paul cites is from our first lesson for today. For him, the innocent expression "one who rises" may have sounded like a reference to the resurrection. In any case, he surely thinks Jesus is the root of Jesse who has extended God's rule now to the Gentiles and in whom the Gentiles can now hope. This final word *hope* returns Paul to the theme with which this lesson began (v. 4). It provides a link to his benediction (v. 13) where the word is used twice more. Either "steadfastness and encouragement" (v. 4) or "joy and peace" (v. 13) might be regarded as worthy goals in their own right, but here they are treated as means to a greater end. Both the steadfastness and encouragement that come from Scripture and the joy and peace that come from believing lead (by the power of the Holy Spirit) to hope.

In short, Paul envisions a community that is united in Christ, united in worship, and united in hope. To be united in Christ means to share the servant mind-set of Christ that places others ahead of ourselves. To be united in worship means to join with others in glorifying God with one voice for the mercy shown to us all. To be united in hope means to recognize the universality of God's promises and the inclusivity of God's reign.

GOSPEL: MATTHEW 3:1-12

This text is a conflation by Matthew of verses from Mark 1:2-8 and verses drawn from the Q source (cf. Luke 3:1-17). The focus is on John the Baptist, who also figures prominently in Matt. 3:13-15; 11:2-19 (from which is taken our Gospel lesson for next week); 14:1-2; 17:9-13; and 21:23-32.

John the Baptist is best known as the forerunner of Jesus; he is the one who calls on people to prepare the way for the Lord's coming. But in Matthew's Gospel he is also Jesus' forerunner in a much more literal sense, as one whose words and deeds actually parallel or foreshadow those later attributed to Jesus. We may note a few obvious similarities between John and Jesus in Matthew's story: (1) The coming of both was foretold by the prophet Isaiah (1:23; 3:3; cf. Isa. 7:14; 40:3). (2) Key elements of John's speech are later echoed by Jesus. John's message, "Repent for the kingdom of heaven is at hand" (3:2) is identical with that of Jesus (4:17), as well as with that of Jesus' disciples (10:7). Both John and Jesus use the epithet "brood of vipers" (3:7; 12:34; 23:33) and both speak of fruitless trees being cut down and thrown into the fire (3:10; 7:19). (3) Both John and Jesus are initially well-received by the masses (3:5; 4:24-25) who regard them both as prophets (11:9; 14:5; 21:11, 26, 46). But in time, both are rejected (11:16-19; 27:20). (4) Both John and Jesus are pictured as being at odds with religious leaders (3:7-10; 9:3) who are not willing to admit that either of the two derive their authority from heaven (21:23-32). (5) Both are eventually arrested (4:12; 26:50) and put to death by the order of Roman authorities (14:10; 27:26).

Even though John is like Jesus in some respects, however, he is clearly subordinate to Jesus (3:14; 11:11) as his own speech declares: Jesus is the more powerful one who will baptize with the holy spirit and fire (3:11). This image has nothing to do with Christian Pentecost, but, rather, connotes the refining and largely destructive judgment (cf. Amos 7:4) that is to come at the end of time. Fire and holy spirit are one: the fiery breath of God, which will consume the wicked. John's role is simply to offer the truly repentant symbolic protection from this conflagration by dipping them in water; Jesus' role will be to unleash the unquenchable fire itself. Top billing at the eschatological judgment should clearly go to him.

John's description of what Jesus will do clashes with what Matthew's reader has been told previously, namely that Jesus will save his people from their sins (1:21). John does not present Jesus as Savior but as Judge, and the judgment he foresees is one of horrible finality—much worse, for instance, than that alluded to in our first lesson for today. Then, the Lord left stumps from which new life might grow (Isa. 10:33—11:1); this time, the ax is laid to the roots.

Jesus the Winnower (v. 12) is such a threatening figure that one may wonder if John has got the right person. Indeed, John himself will be led to wonder this in our lesson for next Sunday (11:2-3)! But John's prophecies are true; only his timing is off. He speaks not of the earthly ministry of Jesus about to commence, but of the eschatological parousia still a ways off (13:37-43; 24:36-44; 25:31-46). Thus, ironic though it seems, the role of John the Baptist according to Matthew's Gospel is not to prepare people for Jesus' first coming but for his second. He is, as the description of his dress in 3:4 indicates, the new Elijah (2 Kings 1:8; cf. Matt. 11:14; 17:12), the one who proclaims repentance in the face of the "great and terrible day of the LORD" (Mal. 4:5-6). Through John the Baptist, God sets in motion preparations for the final coming of Christ even before the earthly ministry of Jesus gets under way. Thus, Matthew grants theological primacy to eschatology, recognizing the extent to which the present is determined by the future. In an analogous way, the church begins its observance of the liturgical year with texts that focus on the end of time: even before we celebrate Jesus' first coming to earth at Christmas, we begin to make preparations for the future advent that should determine our present. These preparations include baptism (v. 6), confession (v. 6), repentance (vv. 2, 8), and the bearing of fruit (v. 8; cf. 7:16-20; 12:33; 13:8, 26; 21:19, 41, 43). But they also include other matters that John does not mention, including attention to those items listed in our second lesson: encouragement, steadfastness, peace, joy, and hope.

REFLECTIONS

The focus for this day continues to be (as last week) on the eschatological power of God's future. Isaiah, Paul, and Matthew all think it is important for us to know the truth about the future; what we believe about what God has planned will surely affect our lives, our decisions, and our morale today.

But whereas Isaiah and Paul seem to regard the future with hope, the words of John the Baptist in our lesson from Matthew describe it much more ominously in terms that many will find threatening. Isaiah describes a time of peace and of universal salvation (11:6-9), while in Matthew, John the Baptist speaks of "coming wrath" (3:7) and of widespread destruction (3:10-12).

Some preachers may be struck by how little gospel there is in today's Gospel lesson. It is true that in Matthew John the Baptist is never described as preaching good news (cf. Luke 3:18), as are Jesus (4:23; 9:35) and his disciples (24:14). Yet the Baptist's vision is an important testimony too, and may be regarded as an expansion on what is only alluded to in Isa. 11:4c-d. His harsh words, furthermore, are directed specifically to those who look for some refuge from judgment that does not demand repentance. These are the ones who need to hear something that will not be good news to them: no such refuge exists.

Taken together, the lessons intertwine threat and promise so as to ✓ provide us with a reliable guide into God's future.

Third Sunday in Advent

Lutheran	Roman Catholic	Episcopal	Common Lectionary
Isa. 35:1-10	Isa. 35:1-6a, 10	Isa. 35:1-10	Isa. 35:1-10
James 5:7-10	James 5:7-10	James 5:7-10	James 5:7-10
Matt. 11:2-11	Matt. 11:2-11	Matt. 11:2-11	Matt. 11:2-11

FIRST LESSON: ISAIAH 35:1-10

Isaiah does it again! Last week we observed that the prophet used the image of new life sprouting from a dead stump in 11:1-10 in contrast to the image of God creating stumps from mighty trees in 10:33-34. The same is true for our first lesson this week: The image of a desert becoming a garden is contrasted with the immediately preceding description of God turning the lovely land of Edom into a wasteland in 34:1-17. Note especially the parallels between 35:4 and 34:8; 35:7 and 34:13; and 35:8 and 34:10.

Our text also shows great similarities with material in Isaiah 40—55 (e.g., "streams in the desert," v. 6; cf. 43:19; 44:3; "pool," v. 7; cf. 41:18; "highway," v. 8; cf. 40:3; "ransomed," v. 10; cf. 51:11). For this reason, most scholars believe it was either written by Second Isaiah or by a still later redactor who copied this prophet's style.

The terms "wilderness," "dry land," and "desert" (v. 1) are all synonyms. They may refer to any desolate or barren region unsuitable for normal habitation. Wild beasts were expected to dwell there (vv. 7c, 9a; cf. Mark 1:13) and by New Testament times the area had come to be thought of as a safe haven for demons (Matt. 12:43). The transformation of such a region into a place where the glory of the Lord could be seen (v. 2) would be truly miraculous but not entirely without precedent. God did after all lead the people through the wilderness for forty years during their exodus wanderings. The supply of water described in v. 6 specifically recalls God's provision for the people during that time (Exod. 17:1-7; Num. 20:2-13). In the New Testament, this setting continues to be significant as the site both of John's baptism and of Jesus' temptation.

God's plan involves renewal of people as well. The blind, deaf, lame, and mute were often considered, like the desert, to be barren and worthless (cf. 2 Sam. 9:8). Sometimes they were thought to be under God's curse (John 9:2), and they were normally excluded from participation in the cult (Lev. 21:16-24). Elsewhere, Isaiah uses blindness and deafness as metaphors for those who do not understand or respond to God (6:10; 28:7; 29:9-10, 18; 30:20-21; 32:3-4) and some of that meaning may be here as well. The overall thought is that there will be no sickness in the new age (cf. 33:24); even those who have been excluded in the past will be able to travel the new pathway to God.

The reference to "fools" in v. 8d may be intended this way as well. Literally the text reads "no fools will stumble upon it (the Holy Way)." This may mean that the highway referred to in 8a will be only for God's people (8c), not for fools or the unclean (8b). The NRSV translation, however, assumes another sense: Even fools will be able to travel this highway without stumbling. The correct reading no doubt depends on whether *fool* refers here to the merely unwise (2 Sam. 24:10; Prov. 12:15; 18:6-7; Eccles. 5:1; 18:6-7) or to the deliberately ungodly (Pss. 14:1; 53:1).

All those who travel the Lord's new highway may be called "redeemed" or "ransomed" (vv. 9-10). The former term was originally used to describe the buying back of property that had been sold, including family members who had fallen into slavery (Lev. 25:25-34, 47-55). The latter was a cultic term used to describe the sacrifice of an animal in the place of a child or of another animal of greater value (Exod. 13:13, 15). Both words came to be used with regard to God's actions for Israel (redeem—Exod. 6:6; 15:13; Pss. 74:2; 77:15; 106:10; Isa. 63:9; ransom—Deut. 7:8; 9:26). In the New Testament, the two concepts merge into one. Jesus gives his life as a ransom (Mark 10:45) and so becomes our redemption (1 Cor. 1:30).

Scholars who attribute this text to Second Isaiah assume the context to be the impending return of captives from Babylon. Scholars who date the text later than this read it with reference to pilgrimages made by Diaspora Jews to the holy city of Jerusalem. In either case, the poetic language indicates that the prophet did not want his meaning to be tied too closely to any one historical setting. By New Testament times, the passage had come to be read as a description of the messianic age, as can be seen in our Gospel lesson for today.

The basic theme is that God comes to God's people in order to prepare God's people to come to God. Verse 4 concludes with a perfect summary of Advent: "God will come and save you!" This word is spoken to people with weak hands and fearful hearts (vv. 3-4; cf. Heb. 12:12). The point is that we don't have to reach God; God comes to us. All infirmities, obstacles, and dangers are removed to enable the weak, the fearful, the afflicted, and the foolish to come to God and experience everlasting joy and gladness (v. 10).

Christians, of course, remember that our Lord Jesus described himself as "the Way" to God (John 14:6) and that this term (the Way) actually became an early self-designation for Christianity (Acts 19:9, 23; 24:14). God offers a way and invites us to come.

SECOND LESSON: JAMES 5:7-10

In this passage we have a collection of sayings on patience. The tenor of these verses is very different from that of the preceding material (5:1-6) and this contrast is best explained by a change of audience. Harsh words of warning are addressed to "rich people" (5:1) and exhortations to patience to the "beloved" (5:7). It is tempting to identify the latter group with the laborers and harvesters who suffer from opposition by the rich (5:4), but the designation is probably more generic than that. James speaks these words to all who await the coming of the Lord with expectancy and hope.

The word used here for patience is *makrothumeō* (literally, "longsuffering"). James provides three examples or models for the encouragement of such patience (although only two are included in our pericope). Each of these relates to a different type of suffering that must be endured.

The first example is that of a farmer who must wait patiently for the harvest (v. 7; cf. Mark 4:26-29). In first-century Palestine, every farmer knew this could be a time of scarcity, a time when the struggle to make ends meet became more acute than ever. No amount of anxiety, however, could make the crops grow faster; one could do nothing but wait on God to send the needed rain (cf. Matt. 5:45; 6:25-27). What type of suffering is envisioned here? Only the normal hardships of life, the expected, almost routine drudgery that life brings to all but the most privileged.

The second example of patience James adduces is that of the prophets who "spoke in the name of the Lord." Here he clearly refers to endurance of a different kind of suffering, namely that of persecution for one's faith. Even though the Old Testament records very few examples of prophets suffering from persecution (2 Chron. 24:20-22; Jer. 26:20-23; 37:11—38:6), traditions that regarded the prophets as martyrs had become very strong by New Testament times (Matt. 23:29-37; Mark 12:1-5; Acts 7:52; Heb. 11:32-38). Jesus taught that people who suffer for righteousness' sake are "blessed" (Matt. 5:10-11), a sentiment with which James apparently agrees (5:11). Such suffering places one in good company (Matt. 5:12).

James offers a third example of patience in 5:11, but our assigned lectionary reading ends with v. 10 and so truncates James' thought. The third example is that of Job, who must endure yet a third kind of suffering—that which comes as a result of sudden and unpredictable calamity. Job loses his home and family to terrorist attacks and to natural disasters (Job 1:13-19), to the kinds of unpredictable and inexplicable catastrophes that insurance companies (like Job's friends) describe as "acts of God."

James does not cite Jesus as an example of endurance, as do other New Testament writers (Heb. 12:1; 1 Pet. 2:21), because the type of suffering endured by Jesus was different from any of the three types described here. According to the gospel tradition, Jesus suffered specifically for our sake, in order to bring about a reconciliation between sinful humanity and God (Rom. 5:6-11; 1 Cor. 15:3). James no doubt regards this type of suffering as too extraordinary for comparison with the trials of his audience.

With reference to the three types of suffering he does have in mind, James simply counsels endurance: "Be patient." But for how long? ". . . until the coming of the Lord" (v. 7). James does not try to explain why such suffering exists, nor does he argue that it can or should be redemptive (but cf. 1:2-4). He simply exhorts us to put up with it, to endure it without grumbling or looking for someone to blame (v. 9), to accept it as the way life is on this side of the parousia.

Throughout history, oppressive people have appealed to texts such as this one to convince the oppressed that they should accept their lot in life rather than trying to improve it. In defiance of such an ideology, Martin Luther King, Jr. wrote his aptly titled book *Why We Can't Wait*. What King opposed, however, was the recommendation of patience as an alternative to reform, and this is certainly not what James intends. Of all the writers in the New Testament, James would be the least likely to extol piety at the expense of justice (cf. 2:15-16). Still, he recognizes that the ultimate hope of the poor is an eschatological one. Only the final, future triumph of God's reign will bring an end to all suffering.

The message of Advent is that this future is "near" (vv. 8, 9). James probably meant near in time (cf. Rom. 16:20; 1 Cor. 7:29-31; Heb. 10:25; 1 Pet. 4:7). Modern Christians may interpret such nearness in ways that transcend the simple temporal dimension: the Lord's coming is near to us if it is close to our hearts and impinges on our lives. The future joy that awaits us can be a source of strength that enables us to endure present trials.

GOSPEL: MATTHEW 11:2-11

The theme of today's Gospel reading is twofold: the identity of Jesus (vv. 2-6) and the identity of John the Baptist (vv. 7-11). We observed in the comments on last week's Gospel lesson that Matthew presents both John and Jesus as proclaimers of God's kingdom (3:2; 4:17) and establishes many similarities between them. This week the identity of these two figures is explored more fully, in ways that define each of the two over against the other.

Jesus' response to John's query (vv. 4-6) alludes to our first lesson for today, as well as to other Old Testament Scriptures (Isa. 29:18-19; 61:1). It is in these allusions rather than in the content of what is said that John will find his answer. That Jesus was healing the afflicted and preaching to the poor was not news; John had already heard about these things (v. 2). In fact, it was the reports of such activities that prompted him to make his inquiry in the first place: "Are you the one who is to come, or are we to wait for another?" (v. 3). These activities, whatever they may be worth, did not in John's mind establish Jesus as the Coming One of whom John had spoken in 3:11-12. By phrasing his response as he does, however, Jesus expects John to recognize that these acts are a fulfillment of Scripture, even if they do not fulfill the particular Scriptures that John has had in mind. In time, of course, all Scripture will be fulfilled. The Judge whom John anticipates will come and "clear his threshing floor" (3:12). But not yet.

As for the identity of John the Baptist, Jesus uses rhetorical images to clarify first who John is not. Whatever else people might say of him (cf. 11:18), no one would ever accuse the Baptist of being a fickle, compromising sort of person who changes direction as easily as a reed blowing in the wind (v. 7). Nor would they regard this camel-clad, locust-eating wilderness dweller (3:1, 4) as a spoiled prince accustomed to the finer things in life (v. 8). No, John was clearly a prophet—and more than that, Jesus adds. He (like Jesus) was one spoken of by the prophets, one whose coming fulfilled a predetermined role in salvation history (vv. 9-10). In fact, Jesus goes on, John the Baptist was the greatest person who ever lived, although even the least in the kingdom of heaven is greater than he (v. 11).

In Matthew's Gospel, the kingdom of heaven is composed of Jesus' disciples and of people who are made disciples through their ministry (28:18). How are such people greater than John the Baptist? First, they are greater in understanding, for Jesus enlightens his disciples concerning the secrets of the kingdom of heaven (13:11) so that they may understand matters hidden even from the prophets (13:17). One such matter is the very point that confounded the Baptist in our lesson for today. None of the prophets, on whose insight John must rely, ever expected a Messiah who would come *twice*. Only after the resurrection of Jesus, when what he has taught is considered in light of what happened, will his disciples be able to understand this essential point. The question of the Baptist posed a false dichotomy. Jesus is the one who was to come, but he is also the one for whom we still must wait.

Jesus' disciples are greater than John in another respect also. Greatness, according to Matthew's Gospel, must be measured in terms of the service one offers to others (20:26). And Jesus' disciples are empowered by Jesus to perform works of ministry that make them the greatest of servants. They do things that John never did: they heal, they deliver people from the power of the devil, and they preach the gospel (10:1, 7-8).

The message of today's text is that it lies within the province of every Christian, every disciple of Jesus, to be "greater than John the Baptist." How? Can we surpass him with regard to devotion, integrity, commitment, or moral character? Perhaps not, but we are already greater in the sense that we stand within the kingdom that he saw only from the outside. On this side of the resurrection, we know God's plan for the future in ways that John could not comprehend, and because we know that plan, we have something to offer our world that he was not able to offer to his. John warned people of judgment, encouraged them to confess their sins, and offered a baptism symbolic of repentance (3:1-12). We are able to speak of salvation, to promise forgiveness, and to baptize in the name of the Father, Son, and Holy Spirit (28:19).

REFLECTIONS

The clash of perspectives presented in our first two lessons for today reads like a dialogue between an idealist and a realist. The bright and glorious picture painted by Isaiah gives way to the more sober advice of James. Into this mix we may also toss the conflicting views of messiahship assumed by the two principal characters in our Gospel lesson for today. John the Baptist looks for a Judge who will condemn the unrepentant (cf. Matt. 3:11-12), but Jesus performs deeds of mercy and preaches good news to the poor (Matt. 11:5).

An overriding theme for the day may be the complexity of God's plans, which seem always to take people by surprise. None of the prophets, not even the greatest of them (i.e., John the Baptist, Matt. 11:11) was able to discern just what God would do or how God would do it. We would be foolish to expect our ideas concerning what is still to come to be devoid of similar surprises.

The way envisioned by Isaiah can no longer be interpreted geo-graphically as a path to Jerusalem but must be read eschatologically as a description of our road to the future. This future *is* glorious. We cannot lose sight of that. But the way to the future is somewhat more treacherous than Isaiah imagined. For now, at least, fools still stumble, lions still prowl, and infirmities often go unmended. The redeemed and the ransomed travel this road but signs of their former captivity remain.

Still, sometimes the future seems almost to have arrived. This happened in the ministry of Jesus and continues to happen in the ministries of his disciples. Sometimes the blind *do* see, the lame *do* walk, the poor *do* hear good news. These events occur because the kingdom of heaven, like the coming of the Lord, is *at hand!* The Greek word *ēggiken*, used in such key Scripture passages as Matt. 4:17 and James 5:8 is intentionally ambiguous. It can mean either "already here" or "soon to arrive." Such eschatological ambiguity describes well the experience of Christians in Advent. At times we are acutely aware of the interim between what is now and what is still to come and then we need to hear James' exhortation to a patience grounded in hope. At other times we may experience a foretaste of the feast to come; then we will want to celebrate with Isaiah the graciousness of God that makes life so worthwhile.

E. B. White, author of the classic *Charlotte's Web*, once said, "I wake up in the morning torn between the desire to enjoy the world and to improve the world. That makes it difficult to plan the day." A similar tension affects Christians who live in the hope of God's salvation. Still, we do well not to make planning our days any simpler by resolving the tension one way or the other.

Fourth Sunday in Advent

Lutheran	Roman Catholic	Episcopal	Common Lectionary
Isa. 7:10-14	Isa. 7:10-14	Isa. 7:10-17	Isa. 7:10-16
Rom. 1:1-7	Rom. 1:1-7	Rom. 1:1-7	Rom. 1:1-7
Matt. 1:18-25	Matt. 1:18-24	Matt. 1:18-25	Matt. 1:18-25

FIRST LESSON: ISAIAH 7:10-14 (15-17)

When the first edition of the Revised Standard Version of the Bible appeared in 1952, a furor arose among some Christians concerning the translation of v. 14 from our first lesson for today. Where the King James Version spoke of a "virgin" being with child, the RSV mentioned only a "maiden." Some people accused the RSV committee of not believing in the virgin birth of Jesus. The argument is an old one. Martin Luther contended, with embarrassing polemic, that only "stubborn, condemned Jews" think Isa. 7:14 can refer to any young woman rather than to one who is a virgin, and he said he would pay them 100 guilders if he was wrong.

The Jews should have collected. Today, virtually all biblical scholars recognize that 'almah means simply "a young woman" (cf. Exod. 2:8; Ps. 68:25; Song of Sol. 1:3; 6:8; another Hebrew word, bethulah, means virgin). The notion of virginity was not introduced into this text until the Septuagint translated 'almah with the Greek word parthenos. Even in the Septuagint, however, Isa. 7:14 does not seem to predict a supernatural occurrence. The point is simply that a woman who is now a virgin will someday conceive and bear a child. This is the only way in which the text was ever read until the remarkable advent of Jesus Christ prompted the evangelist Matthew to look at it in a new light. Matthew's insight is incorporated into our Gospel lesson for today and must be taken into account when the Isaiah passage serves as a text for Christian proclamation. Still, we will begin by considering the text in terms of its original, pre-Christian intent.

The historical context is the crisis precipitated for King Ahaz of Judah by the anti-Assyrian alliance of Syria and Ephraim in 735 B.C. (2 Kings 16; Isa. 7:1-2). Rezin, the King of Syria (also called Aram),

28

and Pekah, the king of Ephraim (also called Israel), have combined forces against Tiglath-Pileser of Assyria, and they are threatening Ahaz with destruction unless he joins them. Ahaz does not wish to set his nation against the might of the Assyrian empire; on the contrary, he decides to side with Tiglath-Pileser and appeal to the Assyrians for help. In the verses preceding our lesson for today (Isa. 7:3-9), the prophet Isaiah suggests a third alternative—political inactivity. Instead of seeking help from the Assyrians or attempting other desperate measures to save himself, Ahaz should trust God for deliverance. This king, so accustomed to taking matters into his own hands, is exhorted to demonstrate his faith in God by doing nothing at all.

Because this advice might be construed as irresponsible or naive, the prophet approaches Ahaz again in today's lesson and offers a sign from God to bolster the poor king's faith. Since the text says it is the Lord who speaks to Ahaz through the prophet (v. 10, cf. Matt. 1:22), we can be certain Isaiah is not presumptuous to make this offer. His invitation to "let it be as deep as Sheol or as high as heaven" is not mere hyperbole either. In the past, prophets have reached into the depths of Sheol to bring the dead back to life (1 Kings 17:17-24), and Isaiah himself will later cause the sun to move backward in the heaven (Isa. 38:7-8). Not all signs from God are miraculous (Gen. 9:12-17; Num. 16:38; 1 Sam. 2:34; 10:1-12; Isa. 20:3-4; Jer. 44:29-30; Ezek. 12:6; Luke 2:12), but some are (Exod. 4:1-9; Judg. 6:17-24, 36-40), and Ahaz is invited to request a miracle if he likes.

Ahaz refuses this offer (v. 12) because he has already decided what he is going to do, and he does not want any signs from God to complicate matters further. His pitiful appeal to Deut. 6:16 reeks of feigned piety and is unconvincing. Of course, modern readers know that in the Synoptic Gospels "signs and wonders" are attributed to false prophets (e.g., Mark 13:22) and that requesting a sign may indicate a lack of faith (Luke 1:18-20) or an evil nature (Matt. 12:38-39; 16:1-4). But Ahaz's refusal ignores the essential fact that this sign is offered through God's own initiative. Actually, the Bible even affirms testing God as a good thing when this testing arises from faith that explores the depths of God's goodness (Mal. 3:10; cf. Ps. 34:8) rather than from a desire to control what God does (Matt. 4:6-7).

Isaiah's response to the king displays an ominous shift of pronouns (cf. "your God" in v. 11 with "my God" in v. 13). For the sake of the "house of David," God will act in spite of Ahaz's intransigence, but

God no longer acts as Ahaz's God. Thus, the sign now offered is a mixed portent of blessing and doom. The immediate threat of the two kings Ahaz fears will soon vanish away (v. 16), but the consequences of trusting in Assyria rather than in God will be harsh (v. 17; cf. Isa. 7:18-25). All this, Isaiah says, will take place before a child yet to be born is able to know good from bad. We don't know exactly what timetable that description would imply, but we do know from history that these predictions were all fulfilled by 722 B.C.

A debate rages among contemporary scholars as to whether the promised child is to be a son of Ahaz (as Jewish tradition attests) or a son of Isaiah himself (on the basis of 8:18; cf. 7:3; 8:3-4). Actually, these efforts at identifying the child's father are somewhat ironic in view of the fact that the text mentions only his *mother*, and even she is (intentionally?) anonymous. For the prophet, the name of the child is the only name that counts.

That name, Immanuel ("God with us"), is the one element in this passage that has overflowed the boundaries of the text to find its way into Christian liturgy, prayers, hymns, and Scripture. For us it has assumed messianic, even incarnational, significance. We do well to remember that in its original context, the promise of Immanuel was a two-edged sword. We may regard the presence of God as a welcome blessing. But to persons like Ahaz, it is an intrusion.

SECOND LESSON: ROMANS 1:1-7

The introduction to what is often considered the greatest of Paul's epistles is so packed with significant references that one could become sidetracked and miss the main point of what Paul is saying. In Greek, the entire lesson for today is all one sentence! The prospect of analyzing the syntax of that sentence or of diagramming it on a blackboard has stymied many a theological student and not a few professors. It may help to realize that the passage appears to be organized into triads, or units of three. The sentence itself has three main parts, and within the first part Paul tells us three things about himself, about the gospel, and about Christ.

The three main parts of the sentence correspond to the conventional formula for opening a letter in ancient times, a formula that is sometimes described as "A to B, Greeting." First, Paul identifies himself (vv. 1-6). Second, he identifies the recipients of his letter (v. 7a). Third, he offers a blessing (v. 7b), which in this case takes the place of a greeting. Looking at these verses with this pattern in mind, one is struck by the disproportionate amount of space given to the first part. Perhaps Paul needs to spend six verses identifying himself because he is not known to this congregation or because he wants to correct misinformation they have received concerning him. As we will see, though, Paul actually devotes most of the space here to talking about the gospel and about Jesus Christ. Like all good witnesses for Christ, Paul knows that what he says about Christ is more important than what he says about himself (cf. John 1:19-27; 3:25-30).

Paul does tell us three things about himself, however, all in the first verse: First, he is a servant (or slave) of Jesus Christ (cf. Gal. 1:10; Phil. 1:1; James 1:1; 2 Pet. 1:1; Jude 1). This image may be drawn from the Old Testament, where Abraham (Gen. 12:1-3; Ps. 105:42), Moses (Josh. 1:2, Ps. 105:26), David (Ps. 89:3; 20), Isaiah (Isa. 6:8-9), and Jeremiah (Jer. 1:4) are all described as God's servants, as are kings (2 Sam. 7:19) and prophets (Jer. 7:25; Dan. 9:6; Amos 3:7) in general. The image might also derive from Paul's familiarity with the teachings of Jesus (e.g., Matt. 10:24-25; 20:27; 23:11). In either case, the thought is not only that Paul serves Jesus but also that Jesus has made Paul a servant of others. In Rom. 6:16-22, Paul will extend the metaphor to include his addressees as well (cf. 1 Cor. 7:22; Eph. 6:6).

The second thing Paul tells us about himself is that he is called to be an apostle. He does not argue the point here, as in Galatians 1–2, but we know from that correspondence that he believes his calling comes directly from Christ rather than through any human institution (Gal. 1:1). His calling is also rather specific: to bring about the obedience of faith among the Gentiles (v. 5; cf. Gal. 2:7-9).

The third thing Paul tells us about himself is that he is "set apart for the gospel." The words *set apart* draw once more on Old Testament imagery (cf. Jer. 1:5) and may also involve a play on Paul's status as a Pharisee (Phil. 3:5; the word means "set-apart ones").

Now that Paul has identified himself, he goes on to tell us three things about this gospel for which he has been set apart: (1) it is "of God"; (2) it was promised beforehand through God's prophets; and (3) it concerns the Son. Paul considers God to be the author of the gospel and Christ to be the content (in grammatical terms, "gospel of God" in v. 1 is a "subjective genitive," while "gospel of his Son" in Rom. 1:9 is an "objective genitive"). In Rom. 1:16 he defines what he means by gospel as "the power of God for salvation to everyone who has faith." Here Paul wants to emphasize that this gospel has been mediated throughout history by the prophets. The medium of oral proclamation has served as the delivery system for God's message that has power to save (cf. Rom. 10:13-17).

Since this gospel concerns "the Son," Paul turns his attention now to telling us three things about this Son: (1) he is descended, physically, from David; (2) he may, however, be declared to be the Son of God on account of the resurrection; and (3) he is the one through whom we have received grace and apostleship. With regard to the first two items (cf. vv. 3b-4), most commentators believe Paul is drawing on a traditional formula, one that espoused the primitive notion that Jesus did not really become God's Son until his resurrection (cf. Acts 2:32-36). Even if this is so, we know that Paul himself did not mean for these words to be construed in such a light. Paul thinks that the resurrection defines in some ultimate sense what it means for Jesus to be the Son of God, but he believes Jesus was already God's Son long before his resurrection (Rom. 8:3; 2 Cor. 8:9; Gal. 4:4; Phil. 2:6-11).

Identifying God's Son as the one through whom apostleship is received returns Paul to the theme of his own calling: to bring about the obedience of faith among Gentiles, including those in Rome to whom he now writes. The expression "obedience of faith" may mean either "obedience that comes from faith" or "obedience, which is faith." In the context of this whole epistle, the latter meaning is probably intended. Faith is the only appropriate response to the gospel, and people who respond to the gospel with faith are obedient to God (cf. Rom. 10:16). It is this obedience of faith rather than outward actions that qualifies God's people to be described as "saints" (v. 7; cf. Rom. 8:27; 12:13; 15:25, 31; 16:2, 15; 1 Cor. 6:1; Eph. 1:15; Col. 1:4; Philem. 5). While apostleship may be a limited calling received only by Paul and a select few, the calling to be saints, to "belong to Jesus Christ" (v. 6), is for all (v. 5).

Some preachers may wonder why this lesson, meaningful though it is, has been chosen for the Sunday before Christmas. Most likely the reason lies in the reference to fulfillment of prophecy in v. 2 and especially in the reference to Jesus' human and divine qualities in vv. 3b-4. The latter passage contains an essential statement regarding what would later be known as the doctrine of the two natures of Christ, a doctrine given further expression in the Nicene Creed (325 A.D.) and the Chalcedonian Definition (451 A.D.). Here, however, Paul understands the link between Jesus' human and divine lineage in light of Easter. Paul did not know the Christmas story; for that perspective we must turn to the Gospel lesson.

GOSPEL: MATTHEW 1:18-25

Matthew's account of Jesus' nativity is read on the last Sunday of Advent to provide transition into the Christmas season. In Matthew's Gospel itself, the full story (1:18—2:23) provides a transition from the prefatory genealogy (1:1-17) to the introduction of Jesus as an adult at the baptism of John (3:1-17). Krister Stendahl once described this story as an "enlarged footnote" on 1:16 because it explains the anomalous reference there to Joseph as the "husband of Mary, of whom Jesus was born" (*The School of St. Matthew* [Philadelphia: Fortress Press, 1968], 102). But the story also prepares implicitly for the explicit identification of Jesus as the Son of God in 3:17.

The focus of Matthew's story is on Joseph, who is identified as a "righteous man" (v. 19; cf. Matt. 13:43, 49; 25:37, 46; 27:4, 19, 24). The NRSV translation of v. 18, which describes Joseph and Mary as engaged but not yet living together, modernizes the story in a way that trivializes the moral quandary this righteous man must face. Actually, betrothal in the ancient world was legally tantamount to marriage and the verb translated here as "live together" refers to the sexual consummation of a marriage relationship. It was common practice in the ancient world for a woman to be legally given in marriage to a man but then to remain in the house of her father until the man had paid her dowry in full. The account in Matthew presupposes this situation. Joseph and Mary are legally wed but have not yet engaged in sexual relations. Thus when Joseph learn his new wife is pregnant, he naturally suspects her of infidelity. Joseph is a righteous man because he is willing to do as the law requires in such an instance and divorce her, but his righteousness exceeds that of the scribes and Pharisees (cf. Matt. 5:20) in that his respect for the law does not cause him to lose sight of the divine quality of mercy (cf. Matt. 5:7; 9:13; 12:7; 23:23). Instead of making a public spectacle of Mary, he resolves to settle the matter as quietly as possible (v. 19). After Joseph learns (vv. 20-23) what the reader already knows (v. 18), namely that this pregnancy is the work of God's Holy Spirit, he demonstrates his righteousness still further by being absolutely obedient to the direction of God (vv. 24-25).

Theological studies regarding this text have focused primarily on the subject of the virgin birth, which in the entire New Testament is mentioned only here and in Luke 1–2. Neither Matthew nor Luke, however, share the fascination of modern theologians with the hows and whys of this event. With regard to "how," Matthew is content to say that it is the work of the Spirit (cf. Luke 1:35) who, after all, created life out of nothingness at the *genesis* (the word translated "birth" by the NRSV in v. 18) of the world (Gen. 1:1; cf. Gen. 2:7). As for "why," Matthew simply believes it was in accord with God's plan to mark Jesus as unique in this manner. A child being born to a virgin is a miracle that is in line with, but also greater than, the Old Testament miracles in which children are born to women who are barren or past the age of childbearing (Gen. 21:2; 30:22-24; 1 Sam. 1:19-20). In the same way, Matthew believes Jesus himself will be in line with, but also greater than, all the heroes of Israel's history. Jesus' status as God's Child is unique, distinct from the status of others who are called children of God (cf. Matt. 5:45; 13:38), distinct even from the status of those whose election to God's work is "from the womb" (cf. Isa. 49:1; Jer. 1:5; Gal. 1:15). We should note that although the virgin birth demonstrates this unique nature of Jesus for Matthew, it is in no way intrinsically necessary. Matthew gives no indication that Jesus had to be born of a virgin in order to be free of the effects of original sin. The notion that being born of a virgin would by itself render Jesus more pure than persons conceived through sexual union disparages God's intended order for creation (Gen. 1:28).

When viewed within the context of Matthew's Gospel as a whole, the virgin birth (which never comes up again) is a less significant theme than the naming of the child, which is used to introduce two prominent themes that will be dealt with repeatedly. The name "Jesus" introduces the theme of salvation. Literally, Jesus (or "Joshua" in Hebrew) means "God helps" or "God saves." The warrior named Joshua in the Old Testament lives up to his name for through him God saves people from their enemies. But this Jesus will be the one through whom God saves people from their *sins* (v. 21). As it turns out, many people in Matthew's story would prefer a Messiah who would save them from Roman occupation or from high taxes to one who will save them from their sins. Similarly, foolish people today often wish that Jesus would save them from this, that, or the other thing, and just leave their sins alone. Our text for today defines Jesus' job description as Savior with precision. He is the one who saves from sin. As Matthew's story continues, we realize he does this by authoritatively forgiving sins (9:5-8), by calling outcast sinners into a new community (9:9-13), and eventually by giving his life as a ransom (20:28) and his blood for forgiveness (26:28).

Matthew says this child will also bear the name "Immanuel," which is derived from our first lesson for today. Although the passage no doubt suggested itself to Matthew on account of the catchword *virgin* used in the Septuagint translation, his appreciation for this text is based mainly on the name Immanuel itself, for it is through this name that he introduces a second major theme for his narrative—the theme of God's presence.

Where and how is God present in our world? Matthew's initial answer to that question is to assert that God is present in Jesus. Although Matthew stops short of actually calling Jesus "God" (cf. John 1:1; 20:28; Titus 2:13; Heb. 1:8), he does say that the birth of Jesus into our world means that God is now "with us." Of course God has been with God's people in some sense throughout history (Num. 23:21; Deut. 2:7; Isa. 43:5; Ezek. 34:30; 37:27; Zech. 8:23), but the presence of God is uniquely manifest through Jesus. People worship Jesus (Matt. 2:2, 11; 14:33; 28:17) even though Jesus himself says that worship is for the Lord God only (4:10). As noted in the "Reflections" section on the First Sunday of Advent, Matthew continues to develop this theme of God's presence throughout his Gospel by noting ways in which Jesus, through whom God is with us, continues to manifest himself to the community (18:5, 20; 25:31-46; 26:26-28; 28:20).

REFLECTIONS

The first three Sundays in Advent all focused in one way or another on the second coming of Christ and on promises of God that are to be fulfilled at the end of time. Today, as we draw near to Christmas, the focus changes to Christ's first coming and to promises that God has already kept.

Both Paul and Matthew believe that ancient prophecies of the Old Testament find their fulfillment in Jesus. Using our first lesson for today as a test case, we can see the sense in which this is true. It would be naive for Christians to assume that Isaiah had Jesus in mind when he delivered his famous prophecy, and it would be arrogant for them to claim that the passage had no legitimate meaning for the people of Isaiah's own day (or for their descendants among the Jewish people of today). Matthew is right, however, to recognize a message in Isaiah's words that transcends their immediate context and allows them to be reapplied with a sense that even the prophet himself never imagined they would have. It is not strange that such a thing should happen. Even today, parishioners often benefit from sermons in ways that the preacher did not intend. The pastor may be surprised to learn that his or her words have spoken to a particular situation with such relevance. If such grace may attend our poor words, how much more might the Spirit drive the text of Holy Scripture to new and timely applications.

We should note again that the accent throughout the Advent season should always include attention to the ways in which Christ comes to us today. The certainty of Christ's presence among us is the foundation for Paul's confidence and the basis for all of the claims he makes in our second lesson for today. The reality of Christ's continued presence among us (cf. Matt. 18:20; 28:20) is also what sustains the concept of Immanuel developed in the other two lessons for today. Both Isaiah and Matthew connect the reality of God's presence to what is the hallmark of the Advent season: hope. The connection is obvious in Isa. 7:14 where the name Immanuel is given as a sign of hope before deliverance is actually accomplished. But the same point is made also by Matthew, who counts the promise that Jesus will save his people from sin (at some point in the future) as an indication that the promise of God's presence has now been fulfilled (vv. 21-22). Significantly, Matthew thinks that hope of salvation alone (as opposed to the actual accomplishment of salvation) should be sufficient for recognition that God is with us. God is present where there is hope.

The Nativity of Our Lord, Christmas Day

Lutheran	Roman Catholic	Episcopal	Common Lectionary
Isa. 9:2-7	Isa. 9:2-7	Isa. 9:2-4, 6-7	Isa. 9:2-7
Titus 2:11-14	Titus 2:11-14	Titus 2:11-14	Titus 2:11-14
Luke 2:1-20	Luke 2:1-14	Luke 2:1-14	Luke 2:1-20

FIRST LESSON: ISAIAH 9:2-7

The verses designated for this pericope are specified according to the way in which they are numbered in the NRSV and most other English translations. A few English versions follow the Hebrew Bible in numbering these verses as 9:1-6.

This passage is appointed for Christmas Day because the child mentioned in v. 6 is often identified with the Christ child (e.g., in the beautiful "For Unto Us A Child Is Born" from Handel's *Messiah*). Originally, the poem was probably written in celebration of either the birth or coronation of a new heir to the Davidic throne. Before long, however, the piece became detached from its original context and was viewed as an expression of the persistent hope that eventually God would raise up a ruler with the qualities here described. In short, the prophet's words came to be viewed as messianic, and those who treasured them looked to the future rather than to the past for their fulfillment.

The poem begins with a reference to people who live in darkness seeing a great light (v. 2). Philip Wheelwright, the preeminent authority on literary and cultural symbolism, says that "of all archetypal symbols there is probably none more widespread and more immediately recognizable than light" (*Metaphor and Reality* [Bloomington: Indiana Univ. Press, 1962], 116). But whereas light is typically a symbol for psychological insight, in the Bible it is more often a metaphor of God's presence (2 Sam. 22:29; Job 29:3; Ps. 27:1; Isa. 42:16; 49:6; 60:1-2, 20) or of God's word (Ps. 119:105; Prov. 6:23). In the New Testament Jesus is said to be the light (Luke 2:32; John 1:4-5; 8:12; 12:35, 46; 2 Cor. 4:6; Rev. 21:23) as are those who believe in him (Matt. 5:14; Eph. 5:8; Phil. 2:15). Here in Isa. 9:2, the specific image is one of grace. The people who have been thrust into deep darkness (8:22) are not responsible for producing this light. The God who controls both light and darkness (Gen. 1:3-5) is solely responsible for bringing about the salvation about to be described.

The content of this salvation is described in vv. 4-5 and its effect in v. 3. To accentuate the connection with today's Gospel lesson, we may say that the content is "peace on earth" (cf. Luke 2:14) and the effect is "great joy for all the people" (cf. Luke 2:10). Specifically, Isaiah describes the peace that God will bring as a release from oppression, a peace grounded in the establishment of justice rather than in the mere cessation of hostilities. Luther interpreted the yoke, bar, and rod of v. 4 as allegorical references to death, sin, and the law. Isaiah surely had more political forces in mind, but in any case, God's victory over these foes will be like that on the day of Midian when Israel's enemies simply destroyed themselves (cf. Judges 6–7). After such a victory, when even the reminders of war have been turned into sources of warmth and light (v. 5), the people will rejoice throughout the nation. This joy will be like that which marks a good harvest, or ironically, like that which their oppressors expressed when enjoying the rewards of war (v. 3).

These hopes are pinned on an individual, a child through whom God will act. Isaiah often relates the concept of deliverance to images involving children, perhaps because he likes the idea of God's power showing itself in the weak and vulnerable (cf. 7:3, 14; 8:1-4, 18; 11:6-8). This child is given four throne names: "Wonderful Counselor" to indicate his wisdom to plan what is right; "Mighty God" to emphasize his power to accomplish those plans; "Everlasting Father" to clarify that his plans and actions will be for the welfare of those he regards as his children; and "Prince of Peace" to specify the content of those plans as being to bring about the establishment of a reign of peace. The final verse of the poem announces that this reign will be endless and affirms once again that all this will be brought about, not through human effort, but through the gracious initiative of God (v. 7).

The high quality of these attributions contributed to the potential for this text to be read in a messianic or eschatological sense. In the Old Testament, the king is often viewed as God's agent but is only called "God" here and possibly in Ps. 45:6-7 (translating the second throne name in v. 6 as "Divine Hero" or "Divine Warrior" ignores the fact that *ēl gibbōr* is clearly used of Yahweh in Deut. 10:17; Isa. 10:21; and Jer. 32:18). Similarly, the king is only rarely called "father" (cf.

1 Sam. 24:11); the adjectives "wonderful" and "everlasting" are usually ascribed to God alone.

Christian interpreters apply all of these labels to the Lord Jesus Christ even though "Wonderful Counselor" is perhaps better suited to the third person of the Trinity (John 14:16, 26; 15:26; 16:7) and "Everlasting Father" only makes sense in light of John 10:30 and 14:8-11. We may do this without shame, for the salvation anticipated in this passage becomes reality through God's action in Christ. We recognize that the messianic age of peace still lies in the future, but we celebrate at Christmas the coming of the child through whom all that Isaiah expected will one day be accomplished.

SECOND LESSON: TITUS 2:11-14

This little passage from Titus is a miniature catechism touching on several aspects of Christian doctrine and life. Originally it provided a theological basis for the advice to households described in 2:1-10. Even if that advice has lost relevance for our current social situation, the basis for such advice set forth in today's text remains valid. The grace of God revealed in Christ has implications for people of every age, sex, and class.

This grace is revealed in two epiphanies, as indicated by the words *appeared* (*epephanē*) in v. 11 and *manifestation* (*epiphaneian*) in v. 13. The Greek terms used in these verses connote a sudden breaking forth of light (as at the dawn) and so recall the image with which today's first lesson began (Isa. 9:2). The references here are to the first and second comings of Jesus Christ.

Our lesson is directed to people who live between these two great manifestations of grace in "the present age" (v. 12). Elsewhere in the New Testament, this present age is described as a time of trouble or as an interim under the dominion of evil powers (Rom. 12:2; 1 Cor. 2:6; Gal. 1:4; 2 Tim. 4:10). Yet during this time, Christians are expected "to live lives that are self-controlled, upright and godly." This triad of expressions points to relationships with self, others, and God, indicating the extent to which grace permeates every aspect of our lives. C. S. Lewis used to say that when people become Christians even their "dogs and cats should be better off for it."

The concern here is for what is sometimes called sanctification, though the lesson does not actually use this term. Rather, it considers "training us to renounce impiety and worldly passions" (v. 12) to be a part of the total salvation brought about through God's grace (v. 11). Jesus gave himself for us (cf. Gal. 1:4; 1 Tim. 2:6) not only to redeem us but also to purify us (v. 14). This notion of purification may draw on the Old Testament image of Moses purifying people by sprinkling them with the blood of the covenant (Exod. 24:8; cf. Heb. 9:14; 1 John 1:7). Because Christ has acted to purify us, we are now "God's own people" (v. 14). an expression that recalls Old Testament references to Israel as God's chosen people (Exod. 19:5-6; Deut. 4:20; 7:6; 14:2; cf. 1 Pet. 2:9). But purification is also linked here to baptism (cf. Titus 3:4-5) since in preparation for baptism and in affirmation of baptism Christians are trained to renounce all that is ungodly. Indeed, the words *renounce* in v. 12 and *purify* (or, literally, "cleanse") in v. 14 probably derive from a baptismal liturgy.

The primary mark of the baptized is not their outward moral character or other-worldliness but their hope (v. 13). Hope, as we have noted throughout the Advent season, means trust in a certain future that has present implications (Rom. 5:2-5; Col. 1:4-5). Hope is grounded in the grace of God that has been revealed and will be revealed, and hope is what provides the basis for Christian sanctification today. Today's first lesson shows Isaiah is confident that "the zeal of the Lord" will take care of the future (Isa. 9:7). Aware of this, Christians may devote their own zeal to good works in the present age (v. 14).

A word should be said about the description of Jesus as "our great God and Savior" in v. 13 of this pericope, one of the only passages in the Bible in which Jesus is actually called "God" (cf. John 1:1; 20:28; Heb. 1:8). As we noted with regard to Isa. 9:6 above, a number of unsuccessful attempts have been made to soften the obvious attribution of divinity to a human being. The text should be read as it stands: Jesus *is* God. He is the Mighty God of Isaiah and he is the great God and Savior of Titus. But he is also, we discover, a very human little baby, wrapped in swaddling clothes and lying in a manger.

GOSPEL: LUKE 2:1-20

Rabbinical commentaries on the Old Testament produced shortly after the time of Jesus sometimes offer insights into the religious and cultural values of that time. In one such writing, a Rabbi bChanina (c. 270) finds a text to be so devoid of meaning and beauty that he must question whether it belongs in Holy Scripture at all. Which text? The Twenty-third Psalm. The rabbi does not care much for this psalm because it compares God to a shepherd, and "no position in the world is so despised as that of the shepherd."

Palestinian shepherds had a difficult and demanding job. They lived out-of-doors most of the time, often pursued a nomadic life-style, and were paid extremely low wages. Even though Abraham, Moses, and David are all described as keeping sheep, by the time of Jesus, shepherding had become a profession most likely to be filled from the lowest ranks of society, by persons who could not find what was regarded as decent work. Society stereotyped shepherds as liars, degenerates, and thieves. The testimony of shepherds was not admissible in court, and many towns had ordinances barring shepherds from their city limits. The religious establishment took a particularly dim view of shepherds since the regular exercise of the latter's duties prevented them from observing the sabbath and rendered them ritually unclean. The Pharisees classed shepherds with tax collectors and prostitutes, persons who were "sinners" by virtue of their vocation.

Such was the status of the people to whom the announcement of Jesus' birth is made in this Gospel lesson. The text says that when these people saw an angel of the Lord standing before them and the glory of the Lord shining all around them they were terrified (v. 9). And well they might be, for they had no doubt been told all their lives that God would eventually come to slaughter the unrighteous. But instead: "good news . . .a Savior!" (vv. 10-11).

Luke's account of the nativity is different from that of Matthew. There Jesus' birth attracts the attention of powerful people, some of whom travel from faraway places to offer him expensive presents (Matt. 2:1-12). In Luke's story, the revelation is to peasants, and to outcast peasants at that. In Luke's Gospel, Jesus is associated with shepherds at his birth, with tax collectors and sinners during his lifetime (5:29-32; 7:34, 36-39; 15:1; 19:1-10), and with criminals in his death (23:32-43). The good news of Christmas is truly for all people (2:10).

This pericope is rich in exegetical nuances, and the standard commentaries on Luke's Gospel have mined these with a luxury we cannot afford here. I will mention only a few items of particular interest:

1. The references Luke provides in vv. 1-3 have proved insufficient for scholars to date the birth of Jesus with precision. Still, they do demonstrate Luke's concern to relate the actions of God to events of

world history (cf. 3:1-2). One reason for doing this is to invite comparison of what he reports of Jesus with what is typically reported of others. We know, for instance, that the various Caesars were often called "Savior and Lord" (cf. v. 11) and that their births were proclaimed as advents that would bring peace on earth (cf. v. 14). The Priene inscription regarding Augustus is particularly instructive for it says that his birthday should mark "the beginning of the good news for the world" (cf. v. 10).

2. The manger is obviously important to Luke; he mentions it three times (vv. 7, 12, 16). Why? A few scholars have suggested that since a manger is a feeding trough, this is Luke's way of presenting Jesus as God's gift of food for a hungry world (cf. 1:53). More plausible, perhaps, is the idea that the key word "manger" would trigger associations with Isa. 1:3, which in the Septuagint reads "the ox knows its master and the ass the manger of its lord." If Luke's readers do not mind being compared to an ass, they may delight in saying that they too know the manger of their Lord (cf. 2:11). The subtle reference to this Isaiah passage may also explain how the ox and ass found their way into our nativity scenes and Christmas carols, since they are not otherwise present in the Christmas story. Placing Jesus in the manger also testifies to his humble beginnings, and the fact that there is no room for him in the inn (v. 7) foreshadows his later career as one who will have "nowhere to lay his head" (9:58).

3. The reference to the shepherds "keeping watch over their flock by night" (v. 8) has apocalyptic symbolism for Luke. Throughout this Gospel, Jesus emphasizes the need for readiness at all times (especially during the night) because the salvation or judgment of God may appear at any time (12:35-40; 17:26-37; 21:34-36; 22:39-46). The shepherds are a good example of persons who keep watch, that is, remain ready for the unexpected.

4. Verse 11 brings three of Luke's favorite titles for Jesus together in a christological nutshell. As Messiah, Jesus is the one who fulfills all the promises made to God's people Israel in the Old Testament (4:21; 24:44). As Lord, Jesus is the one who exercises divine power that overcomes the work of the devil (10:18). In our text for today, Luke stresses that Jesus is both Messiah and Lord from birth (2:11; cf. 1:43; 2:26) even though his identity as Messiah and Lord will not be fully realized until his death and resurrection (Acts 2:32-36). Luke also calls Jesus "Savior," a title not used in the other Gospels except at John

4:42. As Savior, Jesus is the one who sets people free to have the life God wants them to have. He seeks out the lost and restores them to a proper relationship with God (19:10).

5. The word *today* in v. 11 is a favorite of Luke's (cf. 4:21; 5:26; 19:5, 9; 23:43). He uses this word to emphasize the present reality of salvation. Luke writes for people who live between the two epiphanies of grace described in our second lesson for today. He wants them to know that salvation is as available in this present hour as it was in the past or will be in the future. Even today, in between the already and the not yet, those who call upon the name of the Lord will be saved (Acts 2:21; 4:12; 15:11; 16:31).

6. The last part of the angels' song in v. 14 can be interpreted two ways. A literal translation would be "Peace on earth among people whom God favors." The NRSV rendering apparently assumes the concluding phrase to be restrictive: "on earth peace among those whom he favors." Thus, peace is a blessing reserved for those whom God favors (as opposed to those whom God does not favor). But the phrase "whom God favors" may also be taken as simply descriptive: God favors people and so wills peace among them. This latter interpretation is probably more faithful to Luke's interest in the universal character of God's grace. God is for people, not against them.

7. Finally, Luke uses the various characters of his nativity story to demonstrate different responses to the gospel. The shepherds evince what might be regarded as an ideal response: they become witnesses (v. 17; cf. Acts 1:8) and give glory and praise to God (v. 20; cf. 5:25-26; 7:16; 13:13; 17:15, 18; 18:43; 23:47). The people who hear their report are simply "amazed," an ambiguous response that is better than apathy but does not necessarily connote faith (cf. 1:21, 63; 24:41; Acts 3:12). Mary treasures all that she hears and ponders it in her heart (v. 19). Though Mary's response is less exuberant than that of the shepherds, it is probably meant to evidence a deep and abiding faith. Mary is elsewhere portrayed in Luke as an ideal disciple, one who hears God's word and keeps it (8:21; cf. 1:38, 45; 11:28-29). Mary's treasuring and pondering of the word reveals her to be one who holds "it fast in an honest and good heart," and so as one who will "bear fruit with patient endurance" (8:13).

REFLECTIONS

All three lessons appointed for celebrating The Nativity of Our Lord have at their heart a resounding acclamation of grace. In Isaiah's poem we hear that through a child God will bring about the fulfillment of promises so glorious that their accomplishment in our lives will seem like the difference between night and day. In the Epistle to Titus, we hear that God's grace has appeared in Jesus Christ and that the blessed hope we have in him will be augmented by still further manifestations of grace in the future. And in Luke's beautiful Christmas story, we are allowed to participate with the first recipients of grace in the grand announcement of God's favor for all. These lessons have in common a concentration on what God has done, is doing, and will do on our behalf. Grace, sheer grace, is the theme of Christmas. It is no surprise, then, to find in these texts an abundance of words like *light* (Isa. 9:2), *joy* (Isa. 9:3; Luke 2:10), *peace* (Isa. 9:6, 7; Luke 2:14), *hope* (Titus 2:13), and *glory* (Titus 2:13; Luke 2:9, 14).

In many churches, Christmas services are occasions for seats to be filled by persons who have only a marginal commitment to the church. Visiting relatives and reluctant spouses of regular members are apt to show up for this one service, as are members who remain inactive the rest of the year. The sermon, then, ought to be evangelistic in the best sense of the term: a vivid proclamation of the good news revealed to us in Jesus Christ. The preacher's job is to help recreate the experience of that first Christmas night when the glory of the Lord became evident even to people outside the established institutions for religion.

If ever there was a time for preaching *the gospel*, this is that time. If ever there were lessons well-suited for such preaching, these are those lessons.

First Sunday after Christmas

Lutheran	Roman Catholic	Episcopal	Common Lectionary
Isa. 63:7-9	Sir. 3:2-6, 12-14	Isa. 61:10—62:3	Isa. 63:7-9
Gal. 4:4-7	Col. 3:12-21	Gal. 3:23-25, 4:4-7	Heb. 2:10-18
Matt. 2:13-15, 19-23	Matt. 2:13-15, 19-23	John 1:1-18	Matt. 2:13-15, 19-23

FIRST LESSON: ISAIAH 63:7-9

"One hour's misery wipes out all memory of delight," the book of Ecclesiasticus says (11:27). This depressing thought is precisely the sentiment that the author of today's first lesson wants to avoid. He believes times of distress are occasions when the Lord's mercies must be recounted, when memory of delight must be retained. Luther paraphrased the first verse of this lesson as follows: "Because sorrows have begun to attack me, I want to speak about the Lord's blessings, lest I despair."

The three verses that make up this lesson ring with thanksgiving and praise, but they are actually the introductory lines to what must be called a "psalm of lamentation." The full text of this psalm, found in Isa. 63:7—64:12 includes not only remembrance of God's goodness, but also confession of unfaithfulness on the part of God's people and an impassioned appeal for God to act once again. The exact historical setting for the piece cannot be determined for it belongs to that collection of postexilic materials that scholars call "Third Isaiah" (Isaiah 55–56), materials about which very little is known. But this text really is a psalm—we would not have been surprised if we had found it in the Psalter rather than here in the book of Isaiah. The fact that it *is* here reminds us that the line between prophet and poet can be a thin one.

In the Hebrew text, the first word of v. 7 (translated "gracious deeds" in the NRSV) and the last word of v. 7 (translated "steadfast love" in the NRSV) are the same. One word represents both the first and the last thing that this poet would have us remember about God. That word is the Hebrew expression *hesed*, and the fact that we have no equivalent term in English reveals something unfortunate about our culture.

The concept of *hesed* is one of love that (*a*) is based on commitment, and (*b*) shows itself in action. The kind of love that can be described as *hesed* is not affected by the relative loveliness of its object. It is a love that transcends disappointments and failed expectations. Parents may love their children even if those children do not turn out the way the parents might have hoped. Husbands and wives may remain committed to their marriage relationship even when the "romance" is (apparently) gone. The content of such love is not primarily emotional, but behavioral. People love each other (in the sense of *hesed* love) when they treat each other with unselfish kindness and respect.

The word is used here and elsewhere in the Bible to describe God's love for Israel. This love prompted God to act as Savior (v. 8c) both in the Exodus (cf. 63:11) and in the return from exile. One image from those two events has especially captured this poet's attention as a figure of God's grace, namely that of the Israelite women who strapped on their backs the children too small to walk and so carried them across the desert (v. 9d). In the same way, God has been a faithful mother to Israel (cf. Isa. 46:3; 49:15; 66:13).

The poet plays on this image still further by saying that God can identify with the disappointments of parental love as well as with its commitments. As God was saving Israel from distress, this poet imagines God must have been thinking of the future relationship they would someday enjoy together (v. 8). But this was not to be: God's little ones grew up rebellious and unappreciative. God experienced every parent's nightmare, becoming the enemy of one's own children (Isa. 63:10). With images such as these, this poet would shame us into renewal of our relationship with God, a relationship that may have gotten very bad indeed but that can be renewed and sustained because of the *hesed* love God holds for us (cf. Luke 15:11-32).

Textual problems in the first part of v. 9 have made translation of this verse difficult. Where the RSV read "the angel of his presence saved them," most scholars would now recommend the reading in the NRSV: "it was no messenger or angel, but his presence that saved them." The difference accentuates the personal interest that God takes in looking out for the safety and well-being of God's children. This point should not be pushed too far, however, especially in light of the active role played by angels in the rescue of God's son Jesus in our Gospel lesson for today.

SECOND LESSON: GALATIANS 4:4-7

In this Christmas season, it is appropriate to have a text that speaks of God "sending" the Son to us. With the aid of a concordance, one could easily prepare a topical Bible study on this subject. First John 4:9 says that God "sent his only Son into the world so that we might live through him," and the very next verse adds that "God sent his Son to be the atoning sacrifice for our sins." John 3:17 claims that God did *not* send "the Son into the world to condemn the world, but in order that the world might be saved through him." Romans 8:3-4 speaks of God sending the Son so that "the just requirement of the law might be fulfilled in us."

Actually, all of these passages exemplify what scholars call a primitive "sending formula" in early Christianity. Such formulas were used to express the basic purpose of God evident in the Christ event. In our text for today, we hear that God sent the Son "in order to redeem those who were under the law, so that we might receive adoption as children." The redemption that Paul has in mind is specifically redemption *from the law*. In the verses preceding our reading for today, he uses the analogy of legal guardianship to indicate what this means: just as a child may remain under a guardian until a certain time, so we have been under the guardianship of the law. Now, however, the time has come for us to be set free.

In short, Paul believes that Christ has not only redeemed us from the law that condemns us (Gal. 3:13) but also from the law that disciplines or supervises us (Gal. 3:23-25). Christians are free to view the law as their servant rather than viewing themselves as servants of the law (cf. Mark 2:27). We should note, however, that Paul does not envision redemption from the law as an endorsement of self-indulgence (Gal. 5:13). The contrast, rather, is between freedom *as children* as opposed to service *as slaves*. Children have responsibilities as surely as slaves do, but they undertake them with a decidedly different attitude. As children, we serve God and one another out of love, respect, and gratitude rather than simply doing what is required.

We should also note, out of fairness, that for many Jewish people in Paul's day and our own, the law has not been viewed as oppressive or burdensome—as a "yoke of slavery," to use Paul's words from Gal. 5:1. Furthermore, we may be able to find contemporary examples from modern Christian culture for ways in which people become slaves to things intended by God to serve us in our spiritual and religious life. Think, for instance, of the person so devoted to liturgy that he or she cannot worship God unless all the candles are fixed just right and the ministers perform the ritual impeccably. Or think again of that person so devoted to the Bible that his or her concept of community becomes limited to those who interpret particular verses in very specific ways.

The point Paul is making here in Galatians is that the redemption God has accomplished for us in Christ should give us the security and the confidence we need to live as free people. We can use whatever God has given us to the extent that it is helpful, but we will not devote ourselves to anything other than Christ himself. A teenager who was told to put Jesus first in his life once replied, "If I put Jesus first, then he will always have to keep ahead of whatever is second and third. Jesus cannot be first in my life, because Jesus *is* my life." So also with Paul (Gal. 2:20; Phil. 1:21).

God has not only sent the Son to redeem us, Paul continues, but has also sent the Spirit of the Son into our hearts. The Spirit testifies to our adoption as God's children, and through this Spirit we may address God as confidently as did Jesus himself (cf. Mark 14:36). Paul is thinking here of baptism (cf. Gal. 3:25-27), as may be reflected in the Trinitarian language of v. 6 (cf. Matt. 28:19). Whereas some modern Christians emphasize receiving Christ into our hearts through prayer, Paul speaks of God sending Christ into our hearts through baptism. The difference is in the stress on God's sending rather than on our receiving. Both may be necessary, of course, but the Bible contains primitive sending formulas rather than "reception formulas." The accent in the early church was clearly on what God had done.

One reason this text may have been chosen for the Christmas season is its reference in v. 4 to Christ as one "born of woman, born under the law" (one of the only references to Christ's birth anywhere in the epistolary literature). The phrases are intended to highlight Christ's true humanity. To say he was "born of woman" is to affirm that he came into the world in the same way as everyone else (cf. Job 14:1; Matt. 11:11; Paul knows nothing of the virgin birth). To say he was "born under the law" affirms his specifically Jewish identity. The point, simply, is that Christ became *like us* in order to redeem us (cf. Heb.

2:17). This redemption means (negatively) that we are freed from being servants to the law and (positively) that we are freed to live as spirit-filled children of God.

GOSPEL: MATTHEW 2:13-15; 19-23

For the alternative Gospel lesson (John 1:1-18), see the Second Sunday after Christmas.

In discussion of last week's Gospel lesson, we noted that Luke, unlike Matthew, reports Jesus' birth in terms of its effect on peasant people. In Matthew's Gospel Jesus' birth itself is a grand event, eliciting responses from powerful representatives of the Roman and Jewish worlds (2:3-4) as well as drawing the attention of visitors from other lands (2:1-2). But after that it is all downhill. As our lesson for today makes clear, the "glory days" of gold and frankincense and myrrh did not last for long.

The reading for today is organized around movements between four geographical settings that, taken together, relate a downward spiral for Jesus' apparent career and success:

1. *Bethlehem*, where Jesus is at the start of our lesson (cf. 2:1), is the "city of David," a place of great importance in Israel's tradition and God's plan. Even Jesus' opponents knew (or learned) that this was precisely the spot where the Messiah should be born (2:3-6). But from here where would the "King of the Jews" go next? To Jerusalem? No, to Egypt.

2. *Egypt* (vv. 13-15) is a land with ambiguous connotations. It is the place of bondage from which God had to deliver the people in the Exodus. But it is also sometimes a place of refuge (1 Kings 11:40; 2 Kings 25:26; Jer. 43:1-7). Matthew tells the story of the holy family's flight to Egypt with incredible irony. In the Exodus story, babies were slaughtered in Egypt by the wicked pharaoh. But now righteous Jews must flee to Egypt to escape a massacre of infants in their own land (Matt. 2:16-18). Thus, Jesus' detour to Egypt represents a downward turn in the path to glory anticipated by the events of his birth. It is not a detour without precedent; another Joseph, who was also guided by God through dreams, once brought his family here (Genesis 37–50). And, as it turns out, Jesus' sojourn here is a brief one. Soon the family is directed back to Israel (vv. 20, 21), where they belong. But alas! Another problem arises, and they wind up settling in Galilee.

3. *Galilee* (v. 22) was commonly known as "Galilee of the Gentiles" (Matt. 4:15). Though once a part of the northern kingdom of Israel, the land had never really been recovered since its fall to the Assyrians and was now widely populated with "foreigners." The Jews in Judea considered Galilean Jews only a step above Samaritans. Settling here was definitely not a wise career move for anyone who wanted credentials as a Messiah (cf. John 7:41).

4. *Nazareth* (v. 23) is even worse. This little agricultural village with a population of about 500 was so insignificant that at one time some scholars actually denied the place had ever existed. "Can anything good come out of Nazareth?" may have been a proverb of the day. Certainly, these words of Nathanael recorded in John 1:46 would have represented a popular sentiment.

What are we to conclude? That Jesus, who started out so promising, has faded fast? That his "fifteen minutes of fame" are over? No, we cannot conclude this, because Matthew advises us at every turn that everything is transpiring according to God's preordained plan. God directs the holy family at every significant juncture. And even more important, every move they make has scriptural significance: Bethlehem in Mic. 5:2 (cf. Matt. 2:6); Egypt in Hos. 11:1 (cf. Matt. 2:15); Galilee in Isa. 9:1 (cf. Matt. 4:15); and Nazareth in . . . well, actually, no one's sure just where that reference to Nazareth is found (cf. Matt. 2:23), but Matthew thinks it must be in "the prophets" somewhere (the most prominent theories involve the reference to the "shoot (*nezer*) of Jesse" in Isa. 11:1 or to the nazirites in Judg. 13:5-7).

What this portion of Matthew's narrative presents is an unexpected turn in the career of Jesus the Messiah, a turn toward lowliness and humility rather than grandeur and greatness. After leading the reader to believe initially that Jesus would be one before whom kings of the earth would either kneel or tremble (2:3, 11), he now reveals a surprise: Jesus is to be identified, not with the powerful, but with the helpless, vulnerable people of this world. He is to be identified, for instance, with his followers who, like him, will be pursued from town to town (Matt. 10:23).

The forced travels of Jesus and his family provide a powerful symbol for all of the refugees and oppressed people of the earth (the theme of forced travel is also present in a different way in Luke's Christmas story; cf. 2:1-7). A terrible reality of life is that a great many people in many parts of the world are simply at the mercy of political tyrants or unpredictable forces of nature that determine where, when, how, and whether they will live. Our Gospel lesson for today, building in a sense on Paul's simple affirmations that Jesus was "born of woman" (i.e., like us, Gal. 4:4) tells us that Jesus himself was one of these dispossessed ones.

The chief priests would never have thought to look for the Messiah in Nazareth. But then that is the whole point. Jesus was not the kind of Messiah that they or anyone else was expecting.

REFLECTIONS

Nelson Trout, the first African American bishop of any Lutheran church body in America, once said that "in Jesus Christ, God stoops down very low." All three lessons for today testify to a God who "stoops to conquer," that is, who stoops down very low in order to meet us on our own terms, share our humanity, and overcome our sin and stubbornness. In the first lesson, we recount the steadfast love of the God who has lifted us up and carried us in times of distress. In the second lesson, we hear that God sent the Son, born of a woman and born under the law—that is, born a human being and born without privileges, born into the same life that we all live—in order to redeem us from our tendency to live as servants and to create a new potential for us to live as heirs. In the Gospel lesson, we hear of God allowing, even planning for, this Son to suffer the degradations and hardships of an oppressive life so as to be one who identifies with the meek rather than with the powerful.

Another theme reflected throughout all three lessons is that of God's providential care. In the first lesson, we are told how important it is to remember all that God has done for us. Coming as this Sunday does at the end of a calendar year, the day could be devoted to remembrance of what God has accomplished in the congregation and church at large throughout the past year. In the second lesson, God's care is related specifically to the Spirit given in baptism, the Spirit who remains in our hearts and keeps alive the intimacy of our relationship with God. In the Gospel, we witness the meticulous guidance and care with which God provides for the family of Jesus during their time of need.

Parental love as a metaphor for God's grace surfaces in all three lessons also (Isa. 63:8-9; Gal. 4:6; Matt. 2:15). This metaphor, like all figures of speech, has its limits. Some parents do not provide very good models of divine mercy, and even the best will be inadequate in this regard. Still, there is a rich tradition within Israel and the church for understanding ourselves as God's children and further reflection on the meaning of this imagery can lead to deeper appreciation of our liturgical and devotional heritage.

The Name of Jesus (January 1)

Lutheran	Roman Catholic	Episcopal	Common Lectionary
Num. 6:22-27	Num. 6:22-27	Exod. 34:1-8	Num. 6:22-27
Rom. 1:1-7	Gal. 4:4-7	Rom. 1:1-7	Gal. 4:4-7 or Phil. 2:9-13
Luke 2:21	Luke 2:16-21	Luke 2:15-21	Luke 2:15-21

Persons who have access to previously published books in this series of *Proclamation Aids for Interpreting the Lessons of the Church Year* should note that this day is treated in the "Advent/Christmas" volume for every year (not just Series A).

FIRST LESSON: NUMBERS 6:22-27

At the center of this lesson are the well-known words that serve as the closing benediction in most Christian churches today. Some parishioners may be surprised to learn they are from the Bible, as is much of our liturgy. Specifically, these words come from the postexilic "P" material in the Pentateuch, but the benediction itself is much older and was probably used in the first Temple.

Most people today think a blessing is simply a wish, but in biblical thinking it is much more than that. The pronouncement of a blessing was viewed as an actual conferral of that which is mentioned. We might recall the consternation experienced by Esau when his father Isaac mistakenly pronounced the blessing intended for him over his brother Jacob (Gen. 27:1-38).

The blessing here is to be pronounced over a community even though the word *you* in every verse is singular. The thought is that the blessing is for the community as one body, rather than for the particular members of that community as individuals.

The basis for this blessing is provided in v. 27, which also supplies the link to our theme for today. In pronouncing the blessing, God's name is placed on God's people. In fact, the Mishnah informs us that when this benediction was used in the Temple, the sacred name of Yahweh was actually pronounced aloud. But what does it mean to have

53

Yahweh's name placed upon us? Two analogies suggest themselves: marriage and adoption. In patriarchal societies, it is traditional for a woman to take the name of her husband when they marry. This means not only that she belongs to him but also that everything that is his now belongs to her. The woman is given a new identity—her prestige, social status, reputation, and so on will henceforth be determined by the name that is given to her. Even if we reject such a view of marriage as sexist and unfair (and we should!), we might be able to understand our relationship with God in this light. A better example for today's culture may be that of adoption, whereby a parent puts his or her name on a child. Again, the child's identity is in some sense subsumed in that of the parent(s). The child automatically inherits whatever is associated with the family name, including the privileged or disadvantaged status of the parents.

Whichever analogy is used, God must be understood as making a pledge in this familiar benediction. God marries us, or adopts us, or in some other mysterious way puts God's own name upon us so that our identity and status as human beings is now determined by that name. We belong to God, yes, but God also belongs to us and all that God has to offer lies within reasonable expectation for us to receive.

Specifically, the benediction uses the double expression "bless and keep" to convey, positively and negatively, the benefits of bearing God's name. Positively, we are blessed with good things (see Deut. 28:2-14 for a sample list); negatively, we are kept (i.e., guarded) from bad things. We have access, the benediction affirms, to the face of God (vv. 25, 26; the words *face* and *countenance* are the same). In the Bible, God's face is a symbol of God's presence; the word *face*, for instance, was translated *presence* in our first lesson for last Sunday (Isa. 63:9). The image of God's face shining on people is often used in the Psalms (4:6; 31:16; 44:3; 67:1; 80:3, 7, 19; 89:15; 119:135). The assumption is that the light that emanates from God's own being can reach outward to us and so transform our darkness. The image of God's face being "lifted up" is unique, but should be considered over against the frequent references in Scripture to God hiding God's face (Pss. 30:7; 44:24; 104:29). The latter expression means that God is angry, so God showing God's face probably means that God is not angry, but pleased. Hence, the popular liturgical rendering of this verse as "May the Lord look upon you with favor."

The final word of the benediction sums up its entire content: *peace*. The Hebrew word here is *shalom*, which must be interpreted wholistically to include all aspects of life (physical, spiritual, social, etc.). The word implies absolute well-being. This complete well-being is what the benediction intends to confer upon all those who bear the Lord's name.

SECOND LESSON

For Rom. 1:1-7, see the Fourth Sunday after Advent. For Gal. 4:4-7, see the First Sunday after Christmas.

GOSPEL: LUKE 2:21

Those desiring comment on Luke 2:15-20 should see the notes on Luke 2:1-20 for the Nativity of Our Lord, Christmas Day.

In Luke 2:21, we have a one verse report of the circumcision of Jesus, a ritual performed as the law required (Lev. 12:3) on the eighth day after his birth. According to Luke, this was also the time when he was officially given his name (cf. 1:59). For this reason, the church has designated the eighth day after Christmas (sometimes called the "octave of Christmas") for celebrating the Name of Jesus.

The fact that the church celebrates the name of Jesus rather than the circumcision of Jesus accords with the opinion of most scholars that Luke is more interested in the naming than the circumcising. But this conclusion may be too hasty. None of the other Gospels bothers to mention that Jesus was circumcised, and Luke could easily have told this story without including that detail as well (cf. Matt. 1:25). Luke's own writings testify to the great controversies among first-century Christians over the issue of circumcision (Acts 15), as do the epistles of Paul. Against the background of such debates, his report of Jesus' circumcision must be taken as an affirmation of Jesus' solidarity with Judaism (Paul also wants to affirm that Jesus was "born under the law," Gal. 4:4). Gentile Christians in the first century found it easy to ignore this essential Jewishness of Jesus, and Gentile Christians today still find this easy to overlook.

But as we have said, the attraction of this text for today's celebration lies in its reference to the naming of Jesus. Luke's main emphasis in this regard focuses on the fulfillment of God's plan. To be named by

God before birth is a sure sign of one's destiny (cf. Luke 1:31). It is curious, therefore, that Luke does not go on to tell us just why Jesus' name was so significant. Luke seems content simply to tell us that the name was God-given and preordained. He made the same point rather dramatically with regard to John the Baptist (1:13, 57-63).

For development of a sermon we may wish to consider further the meaning of Jesus' name. To do so we may draw on information in Matt. 1:21, information that may just be assumed for Luke's narrative. As we observed in our comments on Matt. 1:21 for the Fourth Sunday in Advent, the name "Jesus" itself is the Greek equivalent of the Hebrew name "Joshua." Either word means "Yahweh helps" or "Yahweh saves." Matthew says Jesus is so-named because he will save his people from their sins. For Luke too the name of Jesus is closely connected with salvation (Acts 4:12).

The word *Jesus* itself describes one important function of the person who bore it: Jesus brings the salvation of God. But a full consideration of the name of Jesus must go beyond mere semantic associations. Matthew, we recall, felt free to give Jesus another name: "Immanuel," which means "God with us" (1:23). This process was to continue; eventually the church would give Jesus a great many names: Alpha and Omega (Rev. 1:8; 22:13), Bread of Life (John 6:48, 51), Bridegroom (Matt. 9:15; cf. Rev. 21:9), Cornerstone (Eph. 2:20); Lamb of God (John 1:29), Word (John 1:1), and so on. To these we might add all of the traditional titles: Savior, Messiah, Lord, Son of God, Son of man, and King of the Jews. And we might also consider those throne names ascribed to the child in Isa. 9:6: Wonderful Counselor, Everlasting Father, Mighty God, and Prince of Peace (see the comments for Christmas Day).

The search for new names did not cease after the New Testament had been written. In the fourteenth century, the mystic Julian of Norwich liked to call Jesus "Mother" because Jesus is the one from whom we are born anew (John 3:3) and by whom we are nurtured with the Sacrament of Holy Communion. In the Ankan culture of Africa, Jesus is often called "Ancestor" to emphasize the preeminence of his standards over all others. In Korea, he may be known as the "Great Yin-Yang," the one whose divine-human nature represents a perfect complementarity of opposites.

The point is that the naming of Jesus did not really stop with the little ritual recorded in our Gospel lesson for today. The church has found the magnificence of Christ to be too great to be contained within any single designation. A variety of images have contributed and continue to contribute to our understanding of Jesus.

REFLECTIONS

The most wonderful thing about the name of Jesus is that this name has been given to us. Just as the Lord God is described as putting God's name on people through the blessing recorded in Num. 6:24-26, so also God puts the name of Christ on us when we are baptized or Christ-ened. The latter term does not really mean that we receive our own name through this event; it means that we receive the name of Christ and that our identity will henceforth be determined by that name. We will be known as "Christ-ian."

To be given the name of Jesus is a wonderful thing because, as the book of Acts reveals, that name confers the presence and power of the One who bears it. The early Christians proclaim repentance and forgiveness of sins in the name of Jesus (Luke 24:47), heal the infirm in the name of Jesus (Acts 3:6-10), and cast out demons in the name of Jesus (Acts 16:18). They do everything in Jesus' name that we would expect to see Jesus himself doing were he still among them. He *is* still among them, present in the name he has given to them.

The name of Jesus is the most wonderful name on earth. Some day, Paul tells us, every knee will bow before the one who bears this name and every tongue will confess that Jesus Christ is Lord (Phil. 2:9-11; cf. 1 Cor. 12:3). And yet we poor mortals have been given this name, and we are allowed—no, *encouraged*—to use it in our prayers (John 14:13; 16:24).

We need to do nothing to receive this name. It is already ours, put on us in our baptism. We may, however, have a great deal to do in order to live up to it. Colossians 3:17 calls upon us to "do everything in the name of the Lord Jesus." Does the world see in those of us who bear the name of Christ what we would want them to see in Christ himself?

Second Sunday after Christmas

Lutheran	Roman Catholic	Episcopal	Common Lectionary
Isa. 61:10—62:3	Sir. 24:1-2, 8-12	Jer. 31:7-14	Jer. 31:7-14 *or* Ecclus. 24:1-4, 12-16
Eph. 1:3-6, 15-18	Eph. 1:3-6, 15-18	Eph. 1:3-6, 15-19a	Eph. 1:3-6, 15-18
John 1:1-18	John 1:1-18	Matt. 2:13-15, 19-23	John 1:1-18

FIRST LESSON: ISAIAH 61:10—62:3

The eleven chapters of the Bible that scholars refer to as "Third Isaiah" (Isaiah 56–66) contain some of the most beautiful poetry in the Old Testament, poetry that was much used by early Christians in coming to understand what God had accomplished in Jesus Christ. Today's lesson actually samples from two separate poems. Isaiah 61:9-10 originally formed the concluding thanksgiving to the oracle presented in chap. 61, while Isa. 62:1-3 formed the beginning of a whole new oracle that runs through chap. 62. The hybrid pericope that results from the combination of these two selections nevertheless works on its own terms, for the two original oracles had themes in common.

The first such theme is the salvation and righteousness of God. This connection is spoiled somewhat in English versions that translate the Hebrew word *tsedeq* differently in one chapter than in another (RSV and NRSV use "righteousness" in Isaiah 61, but "vindication" in Isaiah 62). In Hebrew, the same pair of words (*yeshua* and *tsedeq*) is used in 61:10 and in 62:1. Thus, salvation and righteousness are both the new clothing in which God's people are to be dressed and the light through which God's glory becomes visible to all the world. Both images have New Testament parallels. Paul speaks of Christians "putting on" the Lord Jesus Christ, recalling perhaps the garment given to catechumens at their baptism (Rom. 13:14; Gal. 3:27; cf. Eph. 4:24; Col. 3:10-15). And in the Gospel of Matthew, Jesus says his followers are like a brightly lit city, through whose light people are brought to glorify God (Matt. 5:14-16).

Salvation and righteousness come from God. Elsewhere Third Isaiah tells us that our own righteousness is like a filfthy rag (64:6), but the righteousness with which God clothes us is a garment we would be proud to wear to our own wedding (61:10). The image, accordingly, is one of pure grace. The nations are to see God's own righteousness and salvation when they look at God's people.

Another feature that these two oracles (Isaiah 61–62) have in common is their metaphorical description of God's people as a bride (61:10; 62:5). The problem here is that the people who were responsible for setting the lectionary text have for some inexplicable reason decided to end the reading with 62:3. As a result, our congregations are told that God's people are to be called by "a new name" (62:2), but they are not told what that new name is ("Married" or "My Delight is in Her," 62:4). Preachers who wish to develop this theme, which is introduced in 61:10, should feel free to continue the reading to a more logical stopping point at 62:5. Doing so allows the text to begin with the words "I will greatly rejoice in the Lord" and to end with "so shall your God rejoice over you."

In Isa. 61:10, God's people (symbolized by Zion or Jerusalem) are likened to either a bride or a bridegroom, who is wondrously clothed with the salvation and righteousness of God. In Isaiah 62, God has now assumed the role of bridegroom, and God's people are thought of as God's bride. Elsewhere, Third Isaiah has said that God will rebuild Zion (61:4), bring her prosperity (61:4), and restore her honor (61:7). This new image, however, takes the potential intimacy of Zion's relationship with God to new heights. God's relationship with God's people can be marked not only by faithfulness and mutual respect, but also by something more splendid: delight. Just as New Testament religion rings with proclamations of joy (e.g., Phil. 4:4), so Old Testament religion repeatedly testifies to a God who delights in people (Gen. 1:31; Deut. 10:15) and repeatedly invites those people to delight in God (Pss. 37:4; 40:8). We may recall what Robert Runcie said when, upon being named Archbishop of Canterbury, he was asked by the London press to characterize his own relationship with God. He said, "I enjoy him."

The image of God's people as a bride is also used in Hosea (e.g., 2:19-20), but there the accent is quite different. Israel is portrayed as an unfaithful wife whom God continues to love in spite of her infidelities. In the New Testament, Jesus refers to himself as "the bridegroom" (Matt. 9:15; cf. 22:2; 25:1; John 3:29), and both the church (Eph. 5:25-32) and the "new Jerusalem" (Rev. 21:2, 9) are described as the bride of Christ.

Two other verses in today's lesson present additional images that supplement the pictures we have just discussed. Isaiah 61:11 likens God's goodness to the bounty of the earth upon which we depend but which is produced through processes beyond our comprehension or control (cf. Mark 4:26-29). Isaiah 62:3 likens God's people (Jerusalem) to a beautiful crown that God receives. We are, in other words, God's glory. God gives us righteousness and salvation as our dress (61:10) and receives back all that we have to give—ourselves. A poor trade? God does not think so, but treasures us as the most precious article in the divine wardrobe.

SECOND LESSON: EPHESIANS 1:3-6; 15-18

Once again, the lectionary has chosen to sample from two separate (though related) units of thought rather than offer us one complete passage. Ephesians 1:3-14 presents a prayer of thanksgiving for what God has done in Christ (the entire passage is one long sentence in Greek); Ephesians 1:15-23 is a description of what the writer believes must come next, namely prayer for continued growth in wisdom and in power. The text seems especially appropriate for a Sunday that comes near the beginning of a new calendar year. At this time, individuals and communities often like to reminisce about the past and speculate about the future. A congregation might take time to consider the questions, "What has God done for us in the last year?" and "What can we expect of God in the year to come?" Our second lesson for today may help to guide such consideration.

The prayer that begins in v. 3 uses the familiar "Blessed be . . ." form that is common in the Old Testament (e.g., Pss. 31:21; 72:18) and was adapted by early Christians (2 Cor. 1:3; 1 Pet. 1:3) for liturgical use. Many churches today use a eucharistic prayer that follows this form ("Blessed are you, Lord of heaven and earth . . ."). The concept behind this prayer form assumes a beautiful synchrony between God and people similar to that revealed in the Isaiah lessons for today. People bless the God who has blessed them and rejoice in the God who rejoices over them (Isa. 61:10; 62:5).

The NRSV says that God has blessed us "in Christ with every spiritual blessing in the heavenly places." More in-depth commentaries may help exegetes to unpack all the possible meanings involved in these phrases. We only have room to note the following: (*a*) "in Christ" probably means "through the agency of Christ" but may also mean "by virtue of our union with Christ" (the phrase is used eleven times in vv. 3-14 and some thirty-five times in Ephesians as a whole); (*b*) "every spiritual blessing" would be better rendered "the full spiritual blessing"; God has given us one supreme blessing (Christ) that has many manifestations (adoption, v. 5; redemption and forgiveness, v. 7; salvation and the gift of the Spirit, v. 13; and so on); (*c*) "in the heavenly places" probably refers to the eschatological sphere of the divine (Eph. 1:20; 2:6; 3:10) and the demonic (6:12), a sphere in which battles are fought and victories are won that directly affect the lives of mortals on earth, even though those mortals have no effect on what transpires there. The point here is that the blessing we receive from God in Christ is none of our own doing; it was attained for us through proceedings in which we played no part (cf. Eph. 2:4-9).

Verses 4 and 5 connect this blessing with the biblical doctrine of predestination but in a way that avoids the theological elaboration that sometimes attends that doctrine. No thought is given here to election of individuals, to control of personal destiny, or to what is sometimes called "double predestination" (God appoints some to be saved and others to be lost). Here, what God has done for us in Christ is in keeping with what has been God's intention all along. God has always desired to have a people, and Christ has made it possible for this desire to be fulfilled. Again, what this means for us is that our present relationship with God is wholly and completely dependent upon God's grace (v. 6). We are blessed because God's will is good.

Verse 4 also allows us a glimpse of our future destiny: to be holy and blameless in the eyes of God. Can there be a more precious promise anywhere in Scripture than this? On the basis of this promise, early Christians referred to themselves confidently as "saints" (vv. 1-15). In one sense, the promise has already been fulfilled; on account of the redemption we have through the blood of Christ (v. 7), our sins have been forgiven and we are holy and blameless in God's eyes even now. In another sense, the promise attests to what in the future will become a reality: We will become like Christ when we see him as he is (1 John 3:2). This message of hope is especially relevant today, in what many psychologists refer to as our present "shame-based society."

Most commentators assume that the reference to Jesus as "the Beloved" in v. 6 is a shorthand expression for "Beloved Son of God" (cf. Matt. 3:17; 17:5; Mark 12:6). Another, unexplored possibility is that

Jesus is here presented as *our* Beloved in anticipation of the wife-husband imagery developed in 5:25-33. If this is the case, a connection to our first lesson becomes apparent.

Verses 15-18 indicate that Christians are expected to grow in their appreciation and understanding of what God does for them. The writer notes two areas in which this particular community already excels: faith in the Lord Jesus and love toward all the saints. He does not mention here any specific areas in which growth is still needed, but prays that as God continues to give them wisdom and revelation, they will see these for themselves. Later in the epistle (chaps. 4–6), more direct advice is offered, giving us some idea of what the growing edges may have been for this particular community.

For our own congregations, the main point may just be that growth in grace is always both necessary and possible. As English author and poet George MacDonald used to say, "God is easy to please, but hard to satisfy." Recognition of all that God has done in us and through us and for us makes us thankful, while also encouraging us to new and greater hope for the future. People whose destiny is perfection look forward to each new year with confidence and hope.

GOSPEL: JOHN 1:1-18

For the alternative Gospel lesson (Matt. 2:13-15, 19-23), see the First Sunday after Christmas.

Our Gospel lesson for this week is the prologue to John's Gospel, a beautiful hymn that has been interrupted at two points (vv. 6-8, 15) by parenthetical references to John the Baptist.

The hymn is rich in its allusions to the Old Testament. The initial words *in the beginning* recall the opening of the Hebrew Bible; the continued focus on creation (v. 3) and on light and darkness (v. 5) develop this parallel further (cf. Gen. 1:1-5). In addition, the reference in v. 14 to the Word living (lit., "pitching his tent") among us recalls the traditions of God dwelling in a tent or tabernacle among the people of Israel during their early days (Exod. 25:8-9). According to John's Gospel, Jesus is both the new tabernacle and the new temple (cf. 2:19-22). Just as the glory of God filled the tabernacle (Exod. 40:34) and the temple (1 Kings 8:10-11), so now God's glory has become visible in Jesus (v. 14).

This hymn is most treasured, perhaps, for its stunning Christology, for its cosmic presentation of Jesus as the preexistent Word. The passage testifies to the divinity of Christ with an immediacy matched by only a few other verses in the New Testament (e.g., Titus 2:13; Heb. 1:8). The reference here to "God the only Son" (v. 18) and the bold assertion that "the Word was God" (v. 1) proclaim what for some will become apparent only after Easter: Jesus is God (John 20:28).

We should be careful, however, not to attribute Athanasian, Nicean, or Chalcedonian theology to our fourth evangelist. John is not interested in the metaphysical questions that occupied later generations. John is content to say that Jesus and the Father are one (10:30) without specifying that Jesus is "of one Being with the Father." The unity of Jesus and God envisioned in this Gospel is one of will and action rather than substance. Jesus and God are so closely identified that Jesus reveals what God is like. "Whoever has seen me," Jesus says, "has seen the Father" (14:9).

To speak of Jesus as "the Word of God in human form" (v. 14) is to affirm Jesus as God's own self-revelation to us. Jesus embodies what God wants to say to us. In this Gospel, Jesus' words tell us what God is like and Jesus' deeds show us what God is like. But this is all true only because Jesus himself *is* what God is like. No one has ever seen God (v. 18), but Jesus makes God known to us in a manner that we can see and hear and touch (1 John 1:1). Jesus offers us "hands-on" experience of what God is like.

And just what is God like? God, Jesus reveals, is full of grace and truth (vv. 14, 16-17). The word *grace* used only here in John recalls the Old Testament term *hesed* or "steadfast love" (see our comments for the first lesson on the First Sunday after Christmas). John believes that God is love (1 John 4:16), and the basis for this belief lies in God's own self-revelation of love manifested in Jesus. The word *truth* is used repeatedly throughout this Gospel. John believes that Jesus is the embodiment of the truth that can set people free (8:32; 14:6). Free from what? From the empty, meaningless lives that they live when they do not know the truth about God. When people come to know this truth that God is love, they are able to have abundant life (10:10), eternal life (10:28), life that is filled with light instead of darkness (1:4).

John is aware that some people will reject this truth (vv. 10-11); that rejection itself is used to underscore the graciousness of God. By coming to his own people and laying down his life for his friends, Jesus is able to demonstrate in supreme fashion the inestimable magnitude of God's love for humanity (15:13).

In many ways, these opening verses of John's Gospel are more of an overture than a prologue. They present in summary fashion the key themes of the Gospel as a whole. Jesus is God, and because he is God, he reveals what God is like. The God whom he reveals is a God of grace and truth. Believing in this God enables us to receive grace, to receive in fact an accumulation of "grace upon grace" (v. 16). Receiving Jesus as the self-revelation of God enables us to become God's children and so to begin a familial relationship with the God we have not seen.

REFLECTIONS

Several connections might be noted between the lessons for today, such as the themes of light (Isa. 62:1; John 1:4-5) and glory (Isa. 62:2; John 1:14) repeated in the first lesson and the Gospel. The most prominent theme found throughout all three lessons is grace.

In the first lesson, we are invited to join God's people in rejoicing over all that God has done for us (cf. Isa. 61:10ab with the first lines of the Magnificat in Luke 1:46). God has clothed us with salvation and righteousness, and will, we are told, take us as a bride. God does this out of love and delight.

The second lesson strikes a similar chord. Here we are told that God's good pleasure is to bless us with holiness and to offer us a destiny beyond anything that we could ever have imagined for ourselves. Why does God do this? Simply because it is God's "good pleasure" to do so (Eph. 1:5).

The Gospel lesson tells us that Jesus comes to earth as the Word of God in human form in order to reveal a God of grace and truth. God's love for us is manifest first of all in creation, for God does not despise what God has made. But God's love is further manifest in the sending of a Son who enables us also to become children of God.

Metaphors of intimacy (bride–bridegroom; parent–children) abound in these lessons, for they present God as one who takes pleasure in blessing us, who delights in us and rejoices over us. Jesus has come to reveal the truth about God: God loves us. The words themselves will fit on a bumper sticker, but the implications are anything but simplistic. What shall we do? How do we respond? With rejoicing (Isa. 61:10) and with thanksgiving (Eph. 1:3) and with hearts open to receive all that God wishes to give (John 1:16).